# Senator Robert Carrall

*The pride of blood has a most important and
beneficial influence.*
LETITIA ELIZABETH LANDON (1802–1838)

*Portrait of Senator Robert Carrall.*

# Senator Robert Carrall
## *and*
# Dominion Day

IRENE CRAWFORD-SIANO

*Irene Crawford-Siano*

QUARRY
HERITAGE
BOOKS

Special thanks to: Andrea Roulston, Dorothea Funk,
Gerry & Jill Crawford, Bill Quakenbush, Lindsay Crawford,
Reg Thompson, Dave Mackenzie MP, Kelly-Ann Turkington,
Mary Liley, Jeannette Craddock, Jackie Thompson, Larry
Heath, Arthur B. House Jr., and Terry Lynch.

Cataloging in publication data is available.
ISBN 10 1-55082-350-7
ISBN 13 978-1-55082-350-9

Edited by Bob Hilderley.
Designed and typeset by Laura Brady.
Printed and bound in Canada.
Published by Quarry Heritage Books,
PO Box 1061, Kingston, Ontario K7L 4Y5
www.quarrypress.com

# Contents

# Preface

The first record of the Carroll Family is shown on the Calendar, Westminster, September 23, 1626, when Charles the 1st granted a John Carroll, Esquire, lands in Kings County, Ireland. This 2000-acre grant included castles, manors, tenements, courts, markets, and privilege benefits, but specifically excluded the growing of hemp.

A later record shows that George Carroll, kin to John, had four sons who were expelled from Ireland for political conspiracy. These men, one of whom was named John, settled along the eastern seaboard of the American states, and all were politically active. John had several children, one of who was also named John. Born in March 1753, this John served with General George Schuyler in the American Revolution. A brother Charles signed the Declaration of Independence, the only Catholic to do so, and another relative, Father John Carrall who accompanied them, later became a bishop.

In 1784, unhappy with post revolutionary conditions, John left his wife and children to look after their farm in New York State and traveled on horseback to the backwoods of Upper Canada. He followed an ancient Indian trail from Niagara to the forks of the Askunesippi River, often referred to as the Antler River by the natives. On the banks of this river, which later became known as the Thames, he found land suitable for settlement. He returned home and began negotiations with an agent of the Land and Board, and in 1789 returned with his wife, Matilda, their children and a wagon filled with all their worldly goods. However, John didn't swear the oath of allegiance or petition for land in the Township of Oxford on the River Thames until June 3, 1800. The following spring Matilda gave birth to James, their eighth child and seventh son.

Sometime during these intervening years, John changed the spelling of his surname to Carrall. John and Matilda had eleven children: Abraham, Isaac, Nancy, John J., Jacob, William, Henry, James, Cornelius, Daniel, and Gertrude. Their eighth son, James, married Jane Weir from the Grand River settlement near Burford on April 7, 1819 . The couple had nine children, five boys and four girls. Robert William Weir Carrall, born on February 2, 1839, was their sixth child and fifth son. He trained as a doctor at McGill University, served as a surgeon in the American Civil War, prospected for gold in the Cariboo, became the first representative for the Cariboo District in the British Columbia legislature and a senator in the new Dominion of Canada. He developed a close relationship with Sir John A. Macdonald and introduced the bill to declare as a national holiday the first of July, then called Dominion Day, now called Canada Day. This is his story and part of our national saga. (Based in part on the Obituary of John Carrall in the *Ingersoll Chronicle*, February 23, 1855, available in the Public Archives of Canada.)

Calendar: Westminster. 23rd day of September 1626
Patent and Close Rolls – Chancery – Ireland
of the Reign of King Charles I – Volume 1 Page
163. In keeping of the Records Office – Four
Courts, Dublin Eire.————————

The King to Lord Falkland and the Chancellor:–

Right Trusty and well beloved councillor, we greet
you well: For as much as our trusty and well
beloved subject John Carroll Esquire hath humbly
submitted to the plantation of the Count6y of Ely
O'Carroll in the Kings County in that, our Realm
of Ireland in the time of our late dear father of
blessed memory is of good merit and well affected
in religion, we graciously are pleased. We do
hereby require and authorize you to make an
effectual grant in due form of law with the advice of
learned Counsel there by letter under the great seal
of that, our Realm of Ireland, from us our heirs and
successors, unto the said John Carroll his heirs and
assigns in consideration of all such castles, manor,
lands tenements, courts, markets, fairs, liberties,
privileges, benefits, hereditaments whatsoever
mentioned in the Fiant made in that, our Realm for

a patent to be passed unto the said John Carroll and his heirs in our late dear father's time, to be holden of us-our heirs, and successors by and under rents tenures services and conditions and covenants as in the Fiant are expressed excepting that it shall be lawful for John Carroll to purchase land for him and his heirs of his kindred and others in the County not exceeding in the whole above 2000 acres and also that John Carroll and his heirs be exempted from sowing to hemp. Likewise we are graciously pleased by the letters patent to be made by virtue hereof to grant unto John Carroll £15-8-2 English money rents of Fercall in lieu of chiefries and he shall have such recompense as you think fit for the Castle of Ballandaragh unless it appears to you that he has had satisfaction already. We do hereby require to take order that our Receiver General and vice-Treasurer shall give allowance to John Carroll of the (pound) 40 due by him. For the causes aforesaid and the recommendation of the Commissioners of our Kingdom shall not be made a precedent for others.

THE

# NEW DOMINION

Words & Music by

Arranged by

## W. W. HILL. G. F. WILSON.

DEDICATED TO

## R. W. W. Carrall Esq. M. D.

Cariboo, British Columbia.

✧

MONTREAL. HENRY PRINCE.

# THE NEW DOMINION.

Words and Music by W. W. HILL.

Arr: by G. F. WILSON.

Oh! land of the Ma. ple and Bea.ver we love to hear thy praises A.

.far;  Con.fed.er.a.tion thy strength Do.min.ion thy name, thou

bright and new shining star.  May wisdom pow.er and concord combine, to

*ad lib:* — — — *ritard:*

make thee a gi.ant so grand,  While from o.cean to o.cean thy

*ad lib:* — — —

em.pire extends, in Do.min.ion our own dear father.land.

CHORUS.*

Hail new Do.min.ion thou glo.ri.ous and free Soou

may thy em.pire span from sea to sea.

Dear Sco.tia No.va New Brunswick Red River, and Co.lum.bia British tho'

* The semblance in the Chorus to "Rule Britannia" is intentional.

new. With Can . a . da join'd, say who can e'er sever, A

coun . try and flag firm and true? Thy sis . ter Co . lum . bia whose

*ritard:* _ _ _ _

re . sources are ma . ny would improve under thy fost'ring care. Then

say come with us thou land of the west, we'll make one great fa . ther . land.

CHORUS.

Hail new Do . min . ion thou glo . ri . ous and free Soon may thy em . pire span from sea to sea!

ritard:

ff

# 1. The Family Carrall

Woodstock, Upper Canada: September 25, 1879. On a bluff overlooking the Thames River, golden autumn leaves from the elm and maple trees drifted over the burial site of Dr. Robert William Weir Carrall, as family, friends, and dignitaries from across Canada alighted from their black-draped carriages. They had come to Woodstock to pay their last respects to the Senator for British Columbia and Oxford County's native son.

As the town band played the new Dominion Day anthem, Amelia Carrall, Robert's wife of only four months, wept silently. The anthem had been dedicated to her late husband who successfully maneuvered a bill through parliament creating a national holiday in honor of Canada's birthday on July 1st.

In his eulogy, the Anglican minister pointed out that Dr. Carrall had been many things during his short life: a McGill University trained doctor, American Civil War surgeon, Cariboo miner, Member of Parliament, Canadian Senator, and a son, brother, and husband. He was a man proud of his British heritage and of his ancestors, who had carved a home out of the wilderness in Canada West. Like Dr. Carrall's close friend, Sir John A. Macdonald, Robert believed in Canada's future.

Robert William Weir Carrall was born on February 2, 1839,

at Carroll's Grove, Canada West. He was the fifth son and sixth child of James and Jane Carrall and the grandson of John Carrall, who had trekked through the wilderness to find a safe home for his wife, Matilda, and their family on the banks of what became known as the Thames River.

The Carralls had prospered in Canada West. Robert's father, James, married Jane Weir, a girl from the Grand River Settlement and built a house for his wife on the north side of the Thames River on a lot adjoining his father's property. The house was so grand by the standards of the day that it was only one of three in the County of Oxford that was assessed for taxes.

When James accepted the position of Sheriff on February 10, 1840, for the newly created District of Brock, he located his office in a residence on Mill Street in Woodstock, a street easily accessible from most directions in the County.

The family attended St. Paul's Anglican Church in Woodstock, where they rented a pew five rows behind that of Vice-Admiral Henry Vansittart, the county's most influential man. Church records show that the four Carrall daughters were baptized at St. Paul's Church by Rev. William Bettridge: Sarah Arabella, 21; Maria, 19; Mary Jane, 15; and Anastasia Caroline, 13. It is believed the baptism of the girls became an urgent matter when Marie became seriously ill. She died the following year at age 20. (*Woodstock Monarch*)

It is not known why four of the Carrall boys were baptized at Trinity Anglican Church in Beachville on March 10, 1844, although there was considerable controversy at the time at the parent church. James Alexander, Charles Ingersoll, Robert William Weir, and Henry James — received the "Baptism of such are of Riper Years," the baptismal service of the day. For some reason, John Graham was not included. This very formal service, which meant little to the young boys, was conducted by Rev. William Bettridge, the curate of the parent Anglican church in Woodstock (Old St. Paul's church records).

During Marie's illness, Dr. W. M. John Turquand, a recent graduate of McGill University, became a frequent visitor to the Carrall house. The young doctor had been encouraged to come to Woodstock by both Vice-Admiral Henry Vansittart and Rev. William Bettridge. His many visits made an indelible impression on young Robert, who decided that he wanted to be a doctor when he grew up.

At that time, however, education was a haphazard affair, as documented in the research booklet "Historical Development of the Public Elementary Schools of Woodstock" by Reg Cartmale. Only children whose families could afford to pay school tuition could attend school. All books, which were mostly from the British curricula, had to be purchased and were expensive. Proper school supplies were also scarce. Writing desks were generally long sloping shelves, often as high as the chests of the pupils who sat before them. The seats, eighteen inches to two feet high, were without backs. Although Robert was a sturdy boy, his feet never touched the floor and toward the end of a long day he often sat cross-legged like a tailor.

For several years, George Strauchan B.A., taught the Classics in a room located in the old Central Hotel in Woodstock. Strauchan was considered an excellent teacher, and everyone was delighted when the Governor-General appointed Strauchan to head the first Grammar School in Canada West. An Act of Parliament also provided that 10 students, who were to be selected according to merit from the common schools in the district, could attend the Grammar School, which was equivalent to present-day high school.

Entrance requirements to the Grammar School were stiff, and Robert knew if he wanted to achieve his dream of being a doctor, he had to work hard. He studied the Classics, Latin, Greek, Mathematics, and English, but the only history that was taught in any Canadian school was British history. Strauchan, however, believed that his students should know something about their new country and he encouraged them to write essays about their ancestors.

Robert loved these assignments. He wrote about his grand-father's 1784 journey on horseback from the Mohawk Valley in New York State to the forks of the Askunesippi River, later to be named the Thames River by John Graves Simcoe. Robert wrote about the family's trek through the forest in 1789 and about the building of Carroll's Grove, where his father, James, was born the next spring. He also wrote about his grandfather's problems with an unscrupulous land agent and his grandfather's determination to get his rightful ownership of the land that he had cleared.

Robert wrote a humorous account of the 1801 wedding of a friend of his Uncle John. At that time there were very few ministers in the country and the law stated that only couples married by an Anglican minister were considered legally married. The law was finally relaxed and Magistrates and Justices of the Peace were allowed to marry people, providing there was no Church of England minister within an 18 mile radius. Uncle John's friend wanted Magistrate and Justice of the Peace Thomas Horner to marry him, but Horner lived only 15 ½ miles from an Anglican church. So Horner took the couple 2 ½ miles into the forest where he performed the ceremony with a choir of crows cawing in the background. (*Shenston Gazetteer,* 1852)

History came alive for Robert when he wrote about the War of 1812. Every male from age 16 to 60 had to enroll in the militia, which was divided into active and local regiments. Robert's uncle, Abraham, rode with Captain Hammond Lawrence. His uncle John was a Captain in the Oxford militia, and Robert's father, James, served as a lieutenant in that same militia. Two other Carrall brothers, Jacob and Henry, fought in the Niagara peninsula campaign, where it is believed Jacob and Henry was wounded.

At the time, there were many American sympathizers living in Upper Canada, including Andrew Westbrook, who had purchased a grist mill at Beachville in 1811, just a few miles south of Carrall's Grove. When the war broke out in 1812, Westbrook left a young miller in charge of the mill and with a few other renegades went to the United States, where they became actively involved in the war. Westbrook was later captured but escaped and went on to lead several raiding parties into the Niagara Peninsula. In 1814, he came back to the Thames Valley with a company of Rangers and they burned, looted, ran off the livestock of Westbrook's former neighbors, and even took some of those neighbors as prisoners.

On August 29, 1814, Westbrook and his Rangers burned the mill at Beachville and captured several militia officers, including Captain John Carrall. News of the raid spread quickly, and with the Oxford and Middlesex militia on their heels, Westbrook and the Rangers made a dash to the Byron-Delaware area. Knowing that the militia was close, Westbrook put Captain Carrall on his own pinto horse, slapped his hat on Carrall's head, and, at rifle point, forced Captain Carrall to ride in front of the Rangers. A rescue party, anticipating the route the raiders would take, constructed a barricade across a ravine section of the trail. As soon as the raiders appeared, the militia fired at the leader, believing it to be Westbrook. Captain Carrall was instantly killed. Robert grew up on these stories of the family's patriotism, which were told and retold at family gatherings. His grandfather's love for his British heritage, and his love of this new Colony of Canada, was passed on to his sons and grandsons. These values became deeply ingrained in Robert William Weir Carrall.

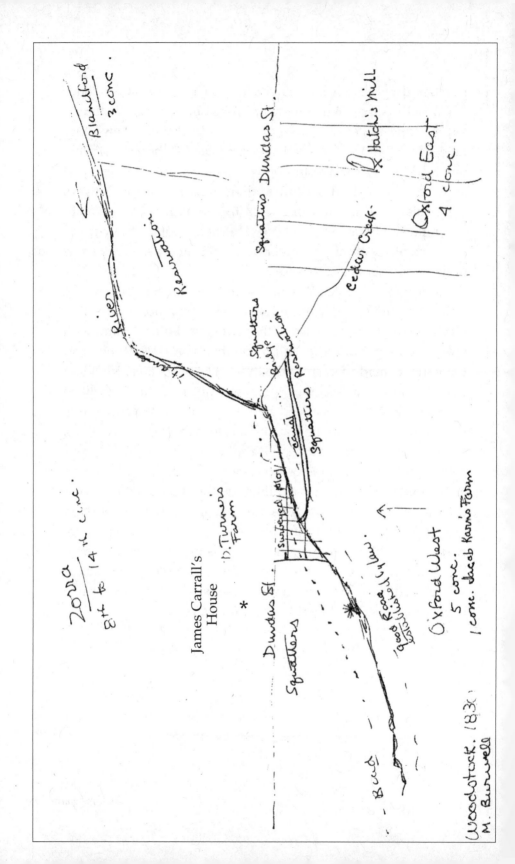

Woodstock. 1830.
M. Burwell

*Plaque at Reservoir Hill in London, Ontario*

# The War of 1812

On August 30, 1814, on this section of Commissioner's Road, a company of Middlesex Militia , led by Captain Daniel Rapelje, ambushed a party of some 70 mounted United States Rangers, guided by former Delaware resident, Andrew Westbrook. The Americans were returning to Amherstburg after a raid on Oxford Township (Ingersoll), where they had taken several prisoners, including 4 officers from the Oxford Militia. Such burn, destroy, and abduction raids were the enemy's military strategy for this part of Upper Canada throughout 1814.

Captain Rapelje became aware of the American presence in the area, and in anticipation, constructed a barricade across the ravine-like section of road. The ensuing ambush routed the Rangers, who fled eastward, leaving casualties on the field. All the prisoners escaped except Captain John Carroll of the Oxford Militia, who was killed.

Funded in partnership with the
London Advisory Committee on Heritage and the Sone Reservoir Hill Group

*Opposite: Rough map by M. Burwell, 1832, showing the Thames River watershed from Woodstock to Beachville.*

*George Strachan, Robert Carrall's most influential teacher*

SOME OF WOODSTOCK'S EARLY TEACHERS.
1. Mr. Dick.   2.   Principal D. H. Hunter.   3.   George Strachan, The Grammar School.   4.
Dr. L. H. Perry, Woodstock's first school teacher.   5.   John Shaw.   6.   Alex. Stewart, forty years a
school teacher.   7.   Hy. Izzard, west end school.   8   L. Stewart, east end school.

*Sheriff James Carrall, Robert Carrall's father*

# 2. Medical Training at Trinity and McGill

Manhood came early to boys in the 1850s. Circumstances sometimes forced boys as young as 13 or 14 to take over the head-of-the-house responsibilities when their fathers died or became disabled. Others married at age 15. Robert Carrall was just ˙ happy youth who kept busy with school and chores. Occasionally, he went hunting or fishing with his grandfather or brothers.

Although James, Robert's father, was available when the family needed him, he was also kept busy with his duties as Sheriff of Oxford County. Despite having an office on Mill Street, people still came to his home in the country to discuss business. It didn't matter if they were rich, poor, bedraggled, or refined; the Carralls always had the welcome mat out.

In the spring of 1851, it was no surprise to the family when James invited the newly-appointed Sheriff of Goderich, John McDonald, to stay for dinner. McDonald had come to Oxford County on law enforcement business, and it was clear during dinner that he was taken with Mary Jane, Robert's sister.

Sheriff McDonald told the Carrall family that he had immigrated to New York State from Inverness, Scotland and then had entered the service of the Canada Company as a surveyor at the age of 33. He had supervised the laying out of the Huron tract from Lake Ontario to Goderich on Lake Huron. Now, at age 51, he was a widower with a nine-year-old daughter, Amelia.

It came as no surprise that Mary Jane and John McDonald were married at St. Paul's Anglican Church in Woodstock on June 21, 1851. Rev. William Bettridge performed the ceremony with the bride's sister, Anastasia and her brother, James, acting as witnesses. Robert, sitting beside his brother Henry in a box-pew near the front of the church, thought that Mary Jane was *smashing* in her high-neck rose taffeta wedding gown. Anastasia, too, was beautiful in her frock of morning-glory blue. Casually glancing across the aisle, Robert suddenly noticed the groom's nine-year-old daughter, Amelia. He was smitten! From that moment on Amelia McDonald had a special place in Robert Carrall's heart.

The next big event in Robert's life came on December 12, 1852 with the arrival of the first Great Western train to Woodstock. With the rest of his family, Robert was dressed in his Sunday best and gathered with hundreds of others at the train station, which was decorated with bunting and flags. Since this was a men only event, the women waited in their decorated carriages lined up along the tracks. At noon, shouts rang out, "There she comes! There she comes!" and minutes later, the first steam-driven train pulled into the Woodstock station. Now considered a man, Robert was allowed to taste a new bubbly wine called champagne. According to Edward Baker's historical montage, *Bits and Pieces*, this was "the first and only time that champagne would be openly served at the Woodstock railway station."

Robert's first train ride came months later when he went to Toronto to enroll at Trinity College. The College was founded in 1851 by John Strachan, the first Anglican Bishop of Toronto and close friend of Rev. William Bettridge. When Trinity finally opened its doors in January 1852, it was able to accommodate 15 divinity students, five medical students, and four students in the arts. It was believed that Rev. Bettridge had entered Robert's name on the enrolment list for future admission. The Carralls were not pleased, however, when they learned that Francis Hincks, their Member of Parliament for Oxford County, had sponsored a bill in 1850 to divest Trinity of its medical and law facilities, leaving that training to the private sector.

Regardless, Trinity College was still a good choice for Robert as he was determined to become a doctor. The college was scheduled to build a botanical garden to grow herbal medicines. The Carrall family had relied over the years on botanical medicines, especially when Maria had been sick. Many botanical remedies had been passed down to the Carralls by non-medical surgeon McCarty, a friend from Grandfather John Carrall's revolutionary days. (Horner file, Woodstock Public Library) Unfortunately, by the time Robert arrived at Trinity College, the school's senate had assigned the responsibility for the construction of the botanical gardens to Trinity's Chairman of Agriculture who, in turn, cancelled the project. The Carralls also learned that several me ical professors, who served as clinical teachers, had to maintain their community practices to supplement their income.

During his third year at Trinity, Robert became disenchanted with the program. While home on vacation in 1856, he talked to Dr. John Turquand, a graduate of McGill University's Faculty of Medicine in Montreal. After their talk, Robert decided to write to McGill to find out if he could transfer and if McGill would allow him credits for the time already spent in the medical program at Trinity College.

In July 1857, Robert transferred to McGill University. The Faculty of Medicine four-year program was considered to be the most advanced in North America. The school had been founded in 1823 by four doctors, three of whom had trained at the renowned Edinburgh Hospital. These doctors believed that all students in their final year should spend time in the wards of a hospital, a novel concept that was gaining appeal in medical circles abroad. In 1852, so that their students would be closer to Montreal General Hospital, the doctors moved the Faculty of Medicine campus to a two-storey brick building on Cote Street. Robert was impressed with McGill's Faculty of Medicine building, which had an anatomy and pathology museum, a large dissecting room, and a 3000-book library. Unfortunately, there were no laboratories for students enrolled in histology, physiology, or chemistry.

As an advanced school, McGill's entrance fees were higher than Trinity College. Robert paid 10 shillings to register and 3 pounds for each course. Fortunately, living quarters were nearby and rent-free. Life at McGill was very different from life at Trinity College. At McGill, students were very much on their own. They were required to get their own information about the hospital, courses, provincial examinations, and licensing. Courses and times were posted:

| | |
|---|---|
| 8 a.m. | Materia Medica |
| 9 a.m. | Institutes of Medicine |
| 10 a.m. | Midwifery |
| 11 a.m. | Surgery |
| Noon | Clinical Medicine and Surgery |
| 2 p.m. | Anatomy |
| 3 p.m. | Practice of Medicine |
| 4 p.m. | Medical Jurisprudence or Medical History, including Botany |
| 7 p.m. | Chemistry |

The medical lectures at McGill were given in the Arts Building and clinical lectures in the operating room amphitheater at the hospital. Because only 30 or so operations were performed each year, all students had to be present. Surgeries were limited because of the threat of infections, about which little was known. Each major course was taught for six months, and there was only one session per year, but not all subjects were taken each year.

Fortunately for Robert, a fellow student, Israel Wood Powell, from Port Dover, Canada West, about 40 miles from Woodstock, became Robert's unofficial guide around the university. Although Powell was actually a year behind Carrall because of Robert's years at Trinity, the two had much in common: both were strong Conservatives and both were members of the Church of England.

Many McGill students were courted by members of the Masonic order, one of the oldest fraternal organizations in the world. Robert knew a bit about freemasonry as his friend and mentor, Dr. John Turquand, was an officer in the King Solomon's Lodge in Woodstock, and his father, James, belonged to Oxford Lodge #76. It is not known whether Robert became a member of one of the Montreal Lodges, but Israel Wood Powell was proposed for membership in February 1858. On April 26, Powell was raised to the Sublime Degree of a Master Mason.

Several times during the year, the medical students were invited to the main campus of McGill University, situated on the outskirts of Montreal. The buildings were surrounded on three sides by open fields and had mountains in the background. The drive was dusty during the summer, muddy during the spring and fall and often snowbound during the winter. One of the professors who drove a horse and sleigh would often take pity on the walking students and give them a ride. Two would get a seat in the sleigh, while others would hang off the side of the sleigh or rode on the runners.

Occasionally, one of the college fraternities would organize a skating party or soccer game for the students. Debates and dramatic skits were often held on weekends, and since these were Robert's favorite pastimes, he always tried to fit them into his already busy schedule.

Records of the Osler Library, McGill University, show that

Robert William Weir Carrall received his degree of Doctor of Medicine on May 3, 1859, at the convocation exercises held at Convocation Hall at the University of McGill College. He placed fourth in his class of 21 and like many of the other graduates, Robert had to spend time in the wards of Montreal General Hospital to fulfil the required hours of practical ward experience required for his degree. Dr. Carrall also used the time to attend postgraduate lectures.

In 1860, Robert returned to Woodstock when his mother, Jane, became ill. He had a surgery on Mill Street in Woodstock, in the same house where his father, James, had his Sheriff's office. Henry Carrall, Robert's brother, acted at his father's clerk and also took on the chore of looking after Robert's calls when he was away from his surgery.

Over the next few months, Jane's condition worsened, and despite all Robert's medical knowledge, he could not save her. Jane Weir Carrall died in December 1861.

Unfortunately, Robert's practice did not flourish as he had hoped. He advertised in *Shenston Gazatteer* and the local paper. He became actively involved with the young people of St. Paul's church. Most professional and business men belonged to a society or fraternity, so Robert joined both Mason fraternities in Woodstock: the King Solomon's Chapter and his father's Oxford Lodge #76. Robert firmly believed in the Mason's basic principles of brotherly love, charity and truth, and he adhered to these principles for the rest of his life.

Because the Carralls were a middle-class affluent family, Robert was surprised to learn there were many poor families living in the area. Old Masonic Records show that on November 13, 1861, the following was placed on their books:

Moved by Brother R. Carrall and seconded by Brother Bell
that the purpose of forming a relief fund, each member
shall pay 25 cents on the regular in the months of January,

April, July and October in each year — and such relief fund to be at the disposal of the W.M. or in the absence of the Senior or Junior warden and bills of relief not be subject to #16.

The two other doctors in the lodge, John Turquand and Henry Smith, supported the motion wholeheartedly.

After the Masonic meetings, the Woodstock doctors liked to talk about new techniques and medicines. Dr. Turquand also liked to reminisce — especially about the time in 1849 when he used anesthetic for the first time. A young man, whose leg had been badly smashed in a tree-cutting accident, would have had to have his leg amputated had Dr. Turquand not rendered him unconscious for an eight-hour operation that saved his leg. Anesthetic was also being used on patients injured in the Civil War that was raging below the border where doctors were desperately needed.

For weeks, Robert's Hippocratic Oath warred against his ancestral loyalties. After much soul searching, Robert decided to close his practice in Woodstock and join the United States Army of the North as a contract doctor.

*Photo of young Dr. Carrall. Advertisement in the Gazetteer*

AND GENERAL DIRECTORY.          227

R. W. W. CARRALL, M. D.,

PHYSICIAN & SURGEON.

RESIDENCE:

WEST WOODSTOCK.

*St. Paul's Church, 1834*

*Bird's eye view of Woodstock in the mid 1860s.*

# 3. Surgeon in the American Civil War

It was a blustery day on December 2, 1862, when Robert William Weir Carrall boarded the train at Woodstock with the destination of Washington, DC, via Buffalo. His practice in Woodstock hadn't grown as he had expected. Robert needed to be needed. He was 23 years old.

At Washington, Carrall went directly to the headquarters of the United States Medical Department, where he signed a contract with the government making him an Acting Assistant Surgeon:

*This contract entered into this $5^{th}$ day of December, 1862 at Washington in the District of Columbia, between Acting Surgeon General of the United States Army and Dr. R. W. W. Carrall of Woodstock in Canada West, witness: That for the consideration hereafter mentioned, the said. Dr. R. W. W Carrall promises and agrees to perform the duties of a Medical Officer, agreeable to the Army Regulations at the department of _____ and to furnish and keep in good order, and accessible at all times, complete sets of amputating, trephining, and pocket instruments, and the said Acting Surgeon General promises and agrees on behalf of the United States to pay or cause to be paid, to the said Dr. R. W. W. Carrall the sum of one hundred dollars for each and every month* *he shall continue to perform the services above stated and one hundred and thirteen dollars per month and transportation in kind when performing service in the field, which shall be his full compensation, and in lieu of all allowances and involvement whatever, and is further agreed that in the case of the said Dr. R. W. W. Carrall be unable to provide the aforesaid instruments they shall be furnished to him by the Medical Department of the Army and the price thereof deducted from his monthly pay. This contract to continue at — six months if not sooner — by the Commanding Officer for the time being the Medical Director or Surgeon General.*

*Sealed and delivered*
*in the presence of*                                    *Acting Surgeon*
                                                         *Chas. C. Lee*
*R.W. W. Carrall*                                       *Ajt. Surgeon*

*Notice of the annulment of this contract, the cause therefore and the date must be forwarded to the Surgeon General.*

After a formal handshake with Adjutant Surgeon Lee, Carrall happily strode off to get a room at either the Metropolitan or Brown Hotel. However, there were no vacancies, and he ended up in a rooming house a few blocks away. Then, it was off to the clothier to be measured for his uniform. The insignia of a medical officer was the letters "MS" embroidered in gold embraced by two olive leaves. On the coat sleeves of an assistant surgeon were two rows of gold braid and on the ends of the coat collar three gold bars extending back one and a half inches.

Contract surgeons were doctors in private practice who agreed to serve in war as assistant surgeons. Their duties were similar to the commissioned surgeons: general patient care, surgical operations, and hospital management. Like Dr. Carrall, most of the contract doctors chose to wear uniforms similar to the uniforms of military surgeons.

On December 12, the same day as his contract arrived at the desk of the office Brig. Gen. W. A. Hammond, the Medical director of the American Army of the North, the following order was received by Robert:

Carrall, R.W.W. A.A.S. USA To report for
duty without delay to Surg. Wm. Clendenin,
USA in charge of Emory Hospital. By CPO
MDO, Washington, Dec. 12. 62

Emory Hospital, which had been a college before it became a hospital, was about a mile east of the capital. It had been named in memory of the education-minded bishop John Emory of Maryland, who had died in a carriage accident in 1835. When it seemed that war between the north and south was inevitable, the governors of the college decided to close the doors of the school. They agreed that when peace took the place of the present public agitation, they would again open the doors.

In April 1861, a Confederate flag was raised at Emory College and recruitment for the Confederate Army began. Shortly afterward the college campus was commandeered by the confederates as a hospital. When the armies of the north moved forward, Emory was taken over by the United States Army of the North.

As soon as he arrived, Dr. Carrall was given a quick tour of the facilities. The hospital complex had a general office, chapel, barracks, twelve wards, a dining room, kitchen, and cook quarters. There were also quarters for the surgeon in charge, officers' quarters, dispensary, linen room, laundry, quarters for two laundresses, quarters for the attendants and guards. There were two store houses and a house for the dead. At the rear of the building, there were stables for the horses.

Nothing, however, prepared Dr. Carrall for the wards of

Emory Hospital. Every bed held a wounded or dying soldier. During his training at Montreal General Hospital, he had seen many people die and experienced the smells of decaying flesh, but nothing had prepared him for this. Dysentery was rampant. Soiled linens were shoved under the bed or in corners — and the cries and moans of the wounded wrenched his heart.

Robert's duties as an Acting Assistant surgeon were to make the rounds of certain wards, change dressings, disperse medicines, diagnose diseases, and sometimes assist with an operation. In actuality, he saw more diseases than wounds: measles, mumps, pneumonia, and typhoid. All flourished in the hospital. He learned that more soldiers were dying from disease than from their wounds on the battlefield, but when he suggested that isolation of contagious diseases could prevent their spread, his suggestion was ignored.

Robert liked the camaraderie of army life, but he hated the close-mindedness of some of the older ranking doctors who wouldn't even consider more advanced and proven methods of medical care, even though the new Medical Director, Brigadier General W.A. Hammond, recommended them.

Time passed quickly, and Dr. Carrall didn't realize it was Christmas morning until the heard a soldier playing a carol on his Jew's-harp. The Jew's harp was a very small, simple musical instrument, held between the teeth and played by striking the free end of a flexible piece of metal with the fingers. It was often carried in a soldier's pocket. In another ward, a patient began playing a carol on his mouth organ. At noontime, turkey miraculously appeared on the menu accompanied by other delicacies. That night, just as the lamps were turned down, the soldiers softly sang *Silent Night*. It was the most meaningful Christmas Robert Carrall had ever experienced.

A new campaign season began in early in 1863. Numerous battles resulted in prisoners being taken on both sides. Robert was heartened when he read a newspaper article which reported

General Robert. E. Lee had released Assistant Surgeon Daniel M. Holt, a northern prisoner, who had been captured on May 8, 1863. Lee had learned that Holt was a fellow mason. (Diary of Daniel M. Holt, MD)

On May 21, 1863, a complaint was lodged against Carrall:

Carrall R.W.W. AAS usa. On duty at Emory hospital, charges against him to be investigated immediately by Surgeon N. R. Mosley, USA in charge of the Hospital, by Dow, MD, Washing., May 21, 63, LB (Some writing unclear)

Surgeon Nathan R. Mosley was a Hospital Inspector under the direction of The United States Medical Department. The positions of medical inspectors were created in 1862 by Congress. All were medical men, half of whom were political appointees. These men were charged with the responsibility for inspections, management recommendations, advice, and the investigations of complaints.

On May 22, 1863, Mosley reported to Surgeon R. O. Abbott, USA, Medical Dir. Dept. of Washington:

I have the honor to report to you that I have investigated the charges preferred by J. E. Dow M.D. against Act. Asst. Surg. R. W.W. Carrall, U.S.A. of Emory Hospital. A.A. Surg. R.W. W. Carrall is an alien — being a resident of Canada. He has been in the service of the United States as A.A. Surgeon since December 12, 1862. He has never taken the oath of allegiance to the U.S. Government, but is perfectly willing to take the oath as contained in the 10th Article of War. I conclude from all the testimony adduced from Medical Officers and others in this Hospital in relation to the specifications in charge 1st – that they are untrue, except so far as relation to the practice of Surgery.

2nd Charge: The testimony of Medical Officers and others, is decidedly in his favor, as to his sympathy for and kind treatment to sick and wounded soldiers. There are no cases of broken back in the house at present, and from the records of the Hospital, I cannot find that there have been any such cases under treatment here. Dr. Carrall states that he has never had under his charge any Confederate prisoners as patients. His prescriptions of medicine for patients in this hospital appear to be in proper doses. Dr. Walsh testifies that in the case of the German spoken of in the charges, that four drops of C-oton oil was administered to relieve obstinate constipation of the bowels with most satisfactory results.

Charge 3 — It appears that A. A. Surg. Carrall has prescribed for himself on two occasions stimulants for the benefit of his health. The regulations of this hospital require that medicines of all kinds for officers and men be prescribed for and regularly dispensed by the officer in charge of the Dispensary.

Very respectfully
Your Obedient Servant
N.R.A. Mosley,
Surgeon U.S.A.
To Surgeon R. O. Abbott, USA
Med. Dir. Dept of Washington.

And with this report the matter was over.

The battle at Gettysburg occurred on July 1, 1863 when the Union Army under General George G. Meade met the Army of the South under General Robert E. Lee. Hospitals were flooded with casualties. Emory had patients in the corridors, and when beds ran out, patients were put on pallets on the floor. Patients were triaged with their wounds: the walking wounded, wounded requiring immediate care, and wounded beyond help. Dr. Carrall had never been as tired in his life as he worked beside the surgeons on a seemingly endless number of casualties.

While on duty one morning a wounded soldier heard an orderly call Robert "Dr. Carrall." He asked if Robert was one of the "Maryland Carrolls." Not waiting for a reply, the soldier continued on to say that he was in the 8$^{th}$ division at Gettysburg under Colonel William Carroll. He added, "The Colonel was a good officer."

Over the next few months, Robert learned that the Carrolls were one of the largest and richest land owners in Maryland. Their home was located at Mount Clare, a beautiful estate with trees and monuments and, of course, slave quarters. Robert's grandfather, John Carrall, had rarely talked about his relatives in the American Colonies. He did mention once that his brother, Charles Carroll, had signed the Declaration of Independence, the only Catholic to do so. He also mentioned that he had a cousin, also named John, who was a priest. In 1776, Father John, Charles Carroll, and Benjamin Franklin had traveled to Canada to gauge the feeling of Canadians to the American cause. (*Benjamin Franklin,* biography by George Canning Hill, 1887)

Finally on July 8, 1863, Robert went on well-earned 10-day leave, returning to duty July 19, 1863. For whatever reason, he left Emory Hospital in September 1863. It was during this period that Brigadier General William Alexander Hammond was removed from office by the Secretary of War, Edwin M. Stanton. He was replaced by Brigadier General Joseph K. Barnes, who continued with most of Hammond's programs.

Then on December 5, 1863, Robert's name appears on the records when he submits a voucher for services at a Hospital in the Field with place of service listed as Washington, DC. Field hospitals were facilities set up quickly behind the lines in any structure that would give shelter to the wounded and dying and provide triage, a system which was introduced in the Crimean War to treat the most severely wounded first.

When battles occurred, the field hospital had to move quickly, sometimes forward, sometimes back. Supplies sometimes got lost or left behind, and the doctors had to be innovative. Chloroform was used sparingly — a piece of cotton gauze was placed over the soldier's nose and an orderly would put a few drops of the chloroform on the gauze, just enough to render the patient unconscious. Cotton threads or horse hair were used to tie off severed limbs, and a good surgeon could amputate a limb in less than 10 minutes. When drugs ran out, doctors used their knowledge of botany to improvise: dogwood became first choice for quinine; American hemlock or motherwort for opium; onions and garlic for poultices; slippery elm and wahoo root and a solution of common salt were used to help pain. Sometimes all that was available as a disinfectant was a solution of salt and water. Beds were made of pallets of straw and pillows made from the down of cattails stuffed in flour and sugar sacks.

Records show also that on December 5, 1863, Robert signed a private physician's contract to perform duties of a Medical Officer, agreeable to "Army Regulations, at the Dept. Of the Gulf." Seven days later, December 12, Robert signed a similar assistant surgeon's contract with United States Army, witnessed by R. O. Abbott, Assistant Medical Director.

There is nothing in the National Archives as to Robert's whereabouts until a report on December 31, 1863. Then, using Marine United States General Hospital New Orleans' stationary, he addressed a letter to Surgeon R. W. Alexander, Medical Director, Department of the Gulf:

I have the honor to Report that I am on duty at the
above named hospital by Order of the Medical
Director, Department of the Gulf. The date of
my contract is December 5, 1863.

This was followed by another report on the same day confirming orders given to him earlier that month:

Transmits Report required by Direction from Medical Director's
Office, December 9, 1864.

The Marines Hospitals of the Gulf were in place before the war. When New Orleans fell to the Union Forces in the fall of 1862, the New Orleans Marine Hospital became part of the Department of the Gulf and had a capacity of 800 beds. (Civil War Medicine)

When Robert had a few hours off from the hospital, he liked to walk through the town, enjoying its bustle and ambience. The balconies, colorful flower boxes, and garlands of Spanish moss that hung from the trees were so different from the sterile, box-like brick houses in Canada West. Someone once told Robert there was a monument to freemasons erected in a New Orleans cemetery, but he couldn't find it. He later learned from a local Catholic priest that the monument was in St. Louis, not New Orleans. The priest's church reminded Robert a little of the Anglican church in Woodstock, where his sister, Mary Jane, had married and where Robert had first seen Amelia, his brother-in-law's daughter — a girl he had never forgotten.

On January 31, 1865, Robert sends another report:

Surgeon R. H. Alexander,
Medical Director,
Department of the Gulf.
    I have the honor to <u>report myself on duty</u> at this
    this hospital under orders from your office dated
    December 31, 1863.

I am very respectfully,<br>
Your obedient servant<br>
R. .W.W. Carrall<br>
Acting Ass't Surgeon

This was followed by another report of January 31, 1865, which simply said, "Transmits monthly report of Station."

Since drugs were always in short supply, doctors often had to use botanical medicines. One of the Assistant Surgeons at the

New Orleans Hospital advertised in the local paper for drugs needed at his hospital. He wanted to buy May apple, blood root, butter nuts, wild cherry bark, fever root, Indian turnip root, skunk cabbage, winter green, and wild ginger. The advertisement in the New Orlean's paper stated that the highest prices would be paid.

Dr. Carrall's report, dated February 28, 1865, suggesed that he has been given new special orders from the Medical Directors Office:

Surgeon R, H. Alexander, USA
Medical Director,
Dept. Of the Gulf.
Sir:
I have the honor to report that I am on duty at this hospital by Special Orders No. 366 Orders Medical Directors Office, Headquarters, Dept of the Gulf, December 30, 1864.

> I am very respectfully,
> Your obedient servant,
> R.W.W. Carrall
> Acting Asst. Surgeon

This was followed by a personal report for the month ending February 28, 1865.

In the absence of medical inspectors, the Medical Directors Office recruited several young doctors to report on the profession concerning the adequacy of surgeons, care of patients, and hospital conditions in the area of Marine Hospital in the Gulf. Robert was one of these recruits. Robert's next report goes directly to the Surgeon General:

April 30, 1865
Brig. General J. K. Barnes,
Surgeon General, U.A.A.
Sir:

Have the honor to report that I am on duty at the Marine, USA
General Hospital, New Orleans, La. as Acting Assistant
Surgeon U.S. Army by Special Order No. 179, dated Medical
Directors Office, New Orleans, La. December 31, 1863.

> I am, Sir
> Very Respectfully,
> Your Obed't Serve't
> RWW Carrall
> A.A.Surg. USA

This was again followed by a personal report dated April
30, 1865. These documents show that Robert was on a special
mission assignment for the Medical Department.

When Robert learned of the assassination of President Lincoln,
he was shocked and saddened and he wanted to quit right then.
But with thousands of men still needing care, Robert stayed at
the Marine General Hospital in New Orleans. He finally annulled
his contract with the United States Army on July 8, 1865.

> Carrall, R. W. W. A.A.S. US.A. To report for duty without
> delay to Surg. Wm Clendenin U.S. Vols in charge of
> Emory Hospital. By O.O. M.D.O. Wash. Dec. 22. '62

> Carrall R. W. W. A.A.S. US.A. on duty at Emory hospital, charges against
> him to be investigated immediately by Surg N.R. Mosely US.V.
> in charge of the hospital. By O.O. M.D.O. Wash. May 21, 62 Lss 68

U. S. General Hospital, "Emory,"

Washington, D. C., May 22d, 1863.

Sir:

I have the honor to report to you that I have investigated the charges preferred by J. E. Dorr M. D. against Act. Asst. Surg. R. W. W. Carrall U. S. A. of Emory Hospital. —

A. A. Surg. R. W. W. Carrall is an alien. — being a resident of Canada, He has been in the service of the United States as A. A. Surgeon since Dec. 12th 1862. He has never taken the oath of allegiance to the U. S. Government, but is perfectly willing to take the oath as contained in the 10th Article of War. —

I conclude from all the testimony adduced from Medical Officers and others in this Hospital in relation to the specifications in charge 1st — that they are untrue except so far as relates to the practice of Surgery. —

2d charge. The testimony of Medical Officers and others is decidedly in his favor, as to his sympathy for and kind treatment to sick and wounded Soldiers. There are no cases of broken back in the house at present, and from the records of the Hospital I cannot find that there have been any such cases under treatment here. —

Dr. Carrall states that he has never had under his charge any Confederate prisoners, as patients. —

His prescriptions of medicine for patients in this Hospital appear to be judicious, and in proper doses. Dr. Walsh testifies that in the case of the German spoken of in the charges, that four drops of Croton oil were administered, to relieve obstinate constipation of the bowels, with most satisfactory results.—

Charge 5th It appears that a. a. Surg Cauall has prescribed for himself on two occasions stimulants for the benefit of his health. The regulations of this Hospital require that Medicines of all kinds for Officers and men be prescribed for and regularly dispensed by the Officer in charge of the Dispensary.

Very Respectfully
Your Obedient Servt.
N. N. Mosely
Surg. U.S.V.
in charge.

To.
Surg. R. O. Abbott U.S.A.
Med. Dir. Dept. of Washington.

Carrall. Robt H. H.
a.a.s.

Hospl or Field

Cont
Dec. 12. 62. —
@ $/1111. or $/113.83

R. B. 4. p. 123.
do    do  231. gives
Washington. D.C. as the place
of service.

Dept of the Gulf.

Dec. 5. 63. — July 8. 65.
@ $/100 or $/113.83
R. B. 5. p. 61.

This Contract, entered into this 1 21st day of December 1863, at Washington , in the State of District Columbia between Surgeon R B Abbott act Med Director of the United States Army, and Dr. R. A. W. Carrall , of Woodstock , in the State of Canada West , witnesseth: That for the consideration hereafter mentioned, the said Dr. R. A. W. Carrall promises and agrees to perform the duties of a Medical Officer, agreeably to Army Regulations, at Washington D.C. or elsewhere and to furnish and keep in good order, and accessible at all times, complete sets of amputating, trephining, and pocket instruments; and the said Surg R. C. Abbott promises and agrees, on behalf of the United States, to pay, or cause to be paid, to the said Dr. R. A. W. Carrall the sum of one hundred dollars for each and every month he shall continue to perform the services above stated, and one hundred and thirteen 83/100 dollars per month, and transportation in kind, when performing service in the field, which shall be his full compensation, and in lieu of all allowances and emoluments whatever;

And it is further agreed, that in case the said Dr. R. A. W. Carrall be unable to provide the aforesaid instruments, they will be furnished to him by the Medical Department of the U. S. Army, and the cost price thereof deducted from his monthly pay. This contract to continue at least three months, if not sooner determined by the commanding officer for the time being, the Medical Director, or the Surgeon General.

Signed, sealed, and delivered }
in the presence of —

R B Abbott
Surg U.S.A.
act Med Director

R A W Carrall

SEAL.

SEAL.

Marine United States General Hospital,

New Orleans La. Dec 31st 1864

Surg. R. H. Alexander USA.
Medical Director
        Dep't of the Gulf

                        Sir

                I have the honor
to Report that I am on duty at the
above named hospital by Order of the
Medical Director Dep't of the Gulf.
The date of my Contract is Dec. 5th 1863

                I am very Respectfully
                Your obedient Servant
                R. W. W. Carrall
                A. A. Surgeon USA.

Marine US Gen't Ent. Hospital
New Orleans, Dec. 31st 1864

R. W. W. Carrall
Act. Ass't Surgeon USA.

Transmits Report required
by Directions from Medical
Directors Office Dec. 9th 1864

Marine United States General Hospital,

New Orleans La., Jan 31st 1865

Surg. R. H. Alexander U.S.A.
Medical Director
Dep't of the Gulf

Sir

    I have the honor to Report
myself on duty at this hospital
under Orders from your Office dated
December 31st 1863

    I am very Respectfully
    Your Obedient Servant
    R. W. W. Carrall
    Acting Ass't Surg. U.S.A.

---

Marine U.S. Gen. Hospital
New Orleans Jan. 31/65

R. W. W. Carrall
Acting Ass't Surgeon U.S.A.

Transmits monthly Report
of station

Marine United States General Hospital,

New Orleans La., Feb. 28th 1865

Surgeon R. H. Alexander U.S.A.
Medical Director
Dep't of the Gulf

Sir

I have the honor to report that I am on duty at this Hospital by Special Orders No. 366 Medical Directors Office, Headquarters Dep't of the Gulf, December 30th 1864

I am very Respectfully
Your Obedient Servant
R W W Carrall
Act. Ass't Surgeon U.S.A.

Marine U.S.Gen. Hospital
New Orleans Feb. 28th 1865

R. W. W. Carrall
Act. Ass't Surgeon U.S.A.

Transmits personal Report for the month ending Feb. 28/65

Marine U. S. A. Genl. Hospital.
New Orleans La  April 30" 1865

Brig Genl. J. K. Barnes.
Surgeon General. U. S. A

Sir:

I have the honor to report that I am on duty at the Marine U. S. A. Genl. Hospital, New Orleans. La. as Acting Assistant Surgeon. U. S. Army, by Special Order No 179, dated, Medical Directors Office. New Orleans, La. December 31" 1863.

I am, Sir:
Very Respectfully
Your Obdt. Servt.
R W Carroll
A. A. Surg. U. S. A.

Marine Genl. Hospital.
New Orleans La. April 30° 65

Carroll. R. W. W.
A. A. Surgeon. U. S. A.

Personal Report

# 4. Cariboo Gold Rush

On July 8, 1865, Robert traded in his medical uniform for a light-weight suit and top hat and boarded a train for San Francisco. Like many soldiers, he found it hard to adjust to peace. He was tired, weary and emotionally drained. His nerves were so on an edge that he couldn't sleep and he drank to keep the cries of the wounded and dying at bay. He was only 26, yet he felt years older.

While he could have gone home to his family in Woodstock, he realized that no one really needed him there. After all, his mother was dead, his father was busy with his work, and his brothers and sister were married. Robert decided he needed a change of place, a place bustling with excitement that could help him forget the last three and a half years.

San Francisco was just such a place. Its taverns, show girls, laughter, and gaiety were solace for the weary soldier. One morning while walking along Montgomery Street, Robert came across the Free Masons, Constantine Lodge #13 sign. He had belonged to the freemasons in Woodstock, Oxford Lodge # 76 and King Solomon's Lodge. He entered and was made welcome by his fellow masons. He met men from other lodges who had also served in the war, some who were interested in politics and some others who were hungering for adventure in some distant place.

Robert heard stories that the Americans were negotiating to purchase Alaska from Russia. He heard about two British Colonies, the Colony of Vancouver Island and the mainland Colony of British Columbia. He heard about the Fraser Valley, Oregon, and the American Northwest. He heard about Australia and New Zealand and their gold rushes.

One afternoon as Robert took a leisurely stroll to Telegraph Hill, a signal station where people could observe the harbor traffic. Once there, he saw two United States Navy ships at anchor. Just the day before he had read that the Navy's fleet of six small wooden vessels had somehow managed to preserve the neutrality of the west coast during the war years. There were several other ships in the harbor as well, but it was the ships flying the red, white and blue flags of the British Navy that caught his attention. Their flags brought nostalgic feelings of home, family, and his British ancestry.

A few hours later, he booked passage on the *Commodore*, a steamboat heading north to the British colony of Vancouver Island. In the steamboat office there had been an advertisement for a doctor to work for the Vancouver Mining and Land Company at its Ladysmith mine. Within the hour, Dr. Carrall had a destination as well as a position.

The *Commodore* was crowded with men of every nationality, all looking for opportunity. There were prospectors wanting to get a head start for spring and land owners and tenant farmers who wanted to build a "rural England" in the fertile land in the valleys of the Rocky Mountains. Men of all ages were seeking their fortune.

Although Robert had sailed on the Great Lakes, this was his first ocean voyage. On the starboard side of the steamer were the snow-capped Rocky Mountains; on the lee side was the endless blue of the Pacific Ocean, where whales swam in the rolling waves. At night, the passengers could hear the distant foghorn of a steamer carrying coal or lumber southward to San Francisco. As the only medical person on board, Robert's services were taxed to the maximum. Despite the steamboat captain's order that there was to be no fighting on board, with space at a premium, numerous fights broke out. Robert's cabin soon became a dispensary and clinic as he stitched blade-slashed faces, splinted broken arms, and doled out powders for sea sickness.

As the steamer neared Seattle, storm clouds rolled in from the north Pacific. Before they reached the Strait of Juan du Fuca, waves almost as big as the ship tumbled over the decks. Passengers were tossed around like driftwood.

As the *Commodore* was steaming through the Strait of Juan du Fuca, the breathtaking scenery caught Robert by surprise. To the southeast, there was Mount Robson with its snow-capped peak glowing pink in the twilight sun. On the British Columbia mainland there were rocky crags and precipices of the Coastal Range and at Victoria and Esquimalt several British ships that lay at an anchor. Elsewhere stately Douglas firs and giant cedars stood tall among the maples, ash, and birch, all dressed in the vibrant colors of early autumn.

The *Commodore* finally docked at Nanaimo, originally a fur trading post owned by the Hudson Bay Company. Now it was a coal mining community owned by a company that recruited miners from Britain, many of whom brought their families with them. Robert was surprised to learn that Nanaimo had a bank, school, jail, literary institute, and, of course, a Hudson Bay store.

He was also delighted to learn that the Freemasons were forming a Lodge in Nanaimo and that a petition had already been sent to England for its dispensation. Since his membership in the Woodstock lodge had lapsed due to military service, Robert was eager to renew it. Records show that a William Carrall became a member of Nanaimo Lodge No. 1090 E.R. in 1865.

Robert joined the Nanaimo Volunteer Rifle Corps and was

elected ensign, giving him the honor of carrying the Union Jack. The corp needed marching music, so he attempted to organize a brass band that would play at municipal and social functions.

The government was asking that militias be formed in communities on the mainland and on Vancouver Island. Many Americans had a dream of controlling the entire Pacific coast from Alaska to Mexico, and they weren't against making an aggressive move to make that dream become a reality. That dream had been temporarily dampened when the Colonial Office in England amalgamated the Colony of Vancouver Island and the Colony of British Columbia. But for some Americans, the dream was reborn when the United States purchased Alaska from Russia. Consequently, the need for a local militia was still valid.

Robert was soon caught up in Nanaimo's social scene. Hostesses were delighted to have a personable bachelor at their table, especially if they had daughters of marrying age. Robert always had a healthy appetite and never said no to a second serving, especially when it was turkey giblets served with thick cream sauce. In addition to looking after his medical responsibilities, he became involved with an amateur theatrical group and enjoyed taking on several acting parts. He also loved to debate, especially subjects that pertained to government and conditions in the coal mines.

Robert was pleasantly surprised one day to meet someone from his hometown of Woodstock, Canada West. Thomas Crosby, a Methodist missionary, had been sent to teach the gospel to the Indian children. After reminisces about home, the two men's conversations drifted to the miners, alcohol, and jail. Robert was appalled by the conditions at the Nanaimo jail when he had been called to treat an incarcerated miner. He immediately appealed to the local magistrate, a fellow Freemason, in an attempt to get improvements, but unfortunately conditions were only minutely improved.

In the spring of 1866, Robert traveled by steamer to Victoria for a few days where he met Dr. Israel Wood Powell, a fellow graduate of McGill University. As well as their medical degrees, the two men had much in common. Both were from small towns in Canada West, both were members of the Church of England, both were freemasons, and both were died-in-the-wool Britishers. Like Robert, Powell had practiced in his hometown (Port Dover) for a short time after graduation. Then, he had decided to go to New Zealand, but en route had ended up in Victoria with a lucrative medical practice. In 1863, Powell was elected to a seat in the Legislature of the Colony of Vancouver Island, and as head of the new Canada Party, he urged confederation with Canada. The two men talked at length about issues, such as free education for children and responsible government, and Robert's political appetite was whetted.

While he was in Victoria, Powell took him to the Birdcages, the Colony of Vancouver Island's parliament buildings. Their architectural design, which was a combination of Elizabethan, Dutch, and Chinese, made them, in his mind, undefinable. Consisting of five buildings, built of wood and brick, with bracketed eaves, dark cream framework and brickwork painted different shades of red, they stood out like something that blew in from foreign soil. Even the colorful buildings of New Orleans couldn't compare with these.

During this visit to Victoria, he also met Dr John Sebastian Helmcken, a distinguished man of about 40 years of age and the son-in-law of Governor James Douglas. Helmcken knew the problems of the miners — long hours, poor working conditions, loneliness, and liquor. As Helmcken once served as a commissioned magistrate he knew how to deal with disturbances among the miners. Now he held the position of speaker of the Colony's legislature.

Robert was also regaled with stories of prosperity and adventure by men from the Cariboo and Fraser River settlement who were wintering in Victoria. They encouraged Robert to leave Nanaimo, advising that if he didn't strike it rich himself, he could always be a doctor to the miners. Robert did return to Nanaimo and the Ladysmith mine, but he had been infected by the lure of adventure and tales of the Cariboo. He decided to leave when his contract ended in December 1866. Later, at a farewell dinner, he was deeply touched when his friends presented him with a book written by his favorite author, Charles Dickens. However, his mind was made up. The lure of the gold fields was too strong.

The Cariboo is a saucer-shaped plateau between the Coast Mountains and the Rocky Mountains, north of the Thompson River. Virtually uninhabited by white men until gold was discovered around Richfield in 1858, it was now the destination of men from all social backgrounds.

The steamer's first stop was at New Westminster, the jumping off place for the Cariboo. While Robert waited for the steamer to load supplies for the miners and dozens of communities upstream, he visited the New Westminster Royal Columbian Hospital. The eight-patient, two-story building was a credit to his medical colleagues, with whom he wanted to keep in touch.

Later as the steamer churned past the islands of the Fraser River delta, Robert got his first look at British Columbia's rich farmlands, which were similar to the farmlands of Oxford County. He became very nostalgic when he saw the mallard ducks and Canada geese feeding along the shoreline — the scene was like those found along the Thames River that flowed past his grandfather's homestead at Carroll's Grove.

Because the paddle-wheeler had a flat bottom and could get in close to shore, it stopped several times on the way up the Fraser River. It was early evening when it reached Yale, a bustling commercial center at the south end of the Fraser Canyon. After a leisurely supper of deer stew and dried apple pie topped with a dollop of whipped cream, Robert retired to a room that he had to share with four other men.

At 3:00 a.m., he and seven others crowded onto the stage coach bound for Spuzzum, the first stop on the 400-mile Cariboo Wagon Road. When one of the passengers started to grumble about the road, another passenger, returning to his ranch on the Omineca plateau, said the man should be grateful they even had a road. Only a few years before the only road north of Yale had been an Indian trail along the walls of the Fraser Canyon. In1862, a contingent of the 172$^{nd}$ Royal Engineers had been sent from Britain to begin the construction of the road from Yale to the Cariboo. The road was built in sections, with the Royal Engineers building the most dangerous sections and civilian contractors building the rest. This particular section of the Cariboo Wagon Road was considered to be the most dangerous, as it had been blasted out of the perpendicular walls of the canyon.

From his coach window seat, Robert could see the morning sun coming up over the mountains, etching their snow-covered peaks in fingers of pale gold. At one point, the stage coach had to pass an oxen-drawn freight wagon train on the narrow road. It was frightening as one misstep could cause the horses and coach to tumble down into the turbulent water of Fraser River.

At Spuzzum, the passengers got a chance to eat and stretch while the stage driver changed teams. Many of them viewed with fear the suspension bridge that spanned the 300 feet across the narrowest part of the river. Robert, however, had confidence in the bridge because he had met the builder, Joseph Trutch, at several political and social gatherings in Victoria. He had been impressed with Trutch's knowledge of engineering, as well as his political acumen.

Less than an hour outside Spuzzum, the stage passed Hell's Gate, the gateway to the narrowing channel of the gorge where the angry Fraser River roared its wrath over the rapids. The next stop was Boston Bar and then on to Lytton, a community which boasted of a resident judge, court house, jail, and a constable. The town had been named after the Secretary of the Colonies and well-known novelist, Sir Edward Bulwar Lytton. (*Ashcroft Journal*)

Then, it was on to Spence Bridge and Ashcroft; and Robert began to lose count of the number of creeks, lakes, wood-bridged gullies, and ravines they crossed. There were also several abandoned shacks, empty sluices, decaying carcasses, and hordes of mosquitoes. But there was something about this land of mountains, glaciers, forests, and plateaus that touched his soul. Robert wondered if this was what his grandfather, John, experienced when he discovered Carroll's Grove on the banks of the Thames River in 1784.

Over the next few days, the stage stopped at Lillooet, 108 Mile House, and 150 Mile House, the latter two named for their distance from Yale. Then, it was on to Soda Creek, Quesnelmouth and Richfield. When the tired horses began to increase their speed, Robert knew they were nearing their destination.

Eight days after leaving Victoria Robert arrived at the Barnard Express depot in Barkerville. Tired and weary from the long hours of travel, he vaguely noticed the frame buildings that lined the half-darkened street. All were built on posts with plank sidewalks connecting them. It's "because of the mud" someone said. Smells of freshly baked bannock from a nearby bakeshop and burning charcoal from a smithy's fire-pit mingled with the loud raucous music from several saloons along the boardwalk.

Securing his luggage, which included his medical bag, Robert crossed the street to a hotel that served meals until 10:00 pm and was crowded with many late-night customers. Within the hour, Robert learned that Barkerville had a hospital, drug store, amateur theater, and a Masonic Lodge, which had empty space on its second floor suitable for a doctor's office. And before finishing his meal, he also had his first patient. The cook in the hotel restaurant had sliced his hand on a butcher knife and needed medical attention.

Robert's first day in Barkerville began with a visit to the Royal Cariboo Hospital, the only hospital north of Kamloops. Dr. John

Bell, an Englishman from Yorkshire, was in charge and assured Robert that there was plenty of work for another doctor. The hospital, built entirely by miners' subscriptions, had opened on October 1, 1863, at the height of the gold rush.

In his first few weeks, Robert treated a young man with a gunshot wound in the leg, set several broken arms, treated two cases of syphilis, and advised a saloon owner with consumption to retire. He was also called upon to testify at a Coroner's jury regarding the death of a man in a mining accident.

When not at the hospital, he went to his cabin on Grouse Creek, which he had bought, sight unseen, from a Bedrock Flume man in Victoria. The cabin, built on posts, was larger than most with two rooms, two windows, a fireplace, and a front porch. It served as his home and office away from Barkerville. It was also a good place to entertain dignitaries who came to the Cariboo, especially with Kelly's bakery nearby.

Robert soon became an accepted part of Barkerville society. Many, like him, were professionals: physicians, lawyers, and military. Most were British. Several belonged to the Masonic fraternity and attended Sunday service at Barkerville's Anglican Church. Robert also joined an amateur theater group, became another voice in the town's Glee Club and became a working member of the Cariboo Benevolent Society helping destitute widows and children and providing meals for sick and hungry miners who were down on their luck.

At a Cariboo Benevolent Society meeting, Robert met a man from his hometown of Woodstock, Thomas H. Pattullo, the first person to buy a site in Barkerville. Before there was a Benevolent Society in the community, Pattullo had raised $615 for a destitute miner dying of consumption to go home to his family.

In addition to their benevolence work, Robert and Tom, besides sharing news from home, enjoyed discussing politics and current affairs, including building a new Dominion of Canada. After one of their discussions, Robert decided to write to Sir John

A. Macdonald, the Prime Minister, whom he called the "great father of the young Dominion." Carrall eloquently expressed his views on the Colony of British Columbia joining confederation. Many Americans, he said, believed that the annexation of British Columbia was a very plausible step in taking control of the entire west coast of North America. And after more than three years as a contract doctor in the United States Army of the North, he knew first- hand what a country divided against *itself* could do to its people.

The Prime Minister was impressed with Robert's zealousness for confederation, and in his response Macdonald urged him "to keep the Union fire alight until it burns over the whole country." This was the beginning of a friendship that would last Robert's lifetime. R.W., as many of his friends called him, loved his life here in the Cariboo. It was raw and raucous, especially at night when the saloons were crowded with miners. One saloon featured the "hurdy-gurdy girls," German dancers brought to the Cariboo by Fanny Bendixon, a buxom, eccentric entrepreneur from San Francisco. The girls wore grotesque, yet appealing costumes of red print skirts and half-mourning headdresses, which looked like a turkey's topknot. Like most of the miners, the good doctor loved to dance, and it was an accepted fact that the man who could hoist his 'gal' the highest was considered the best dancer. R. W. tried, but never quite succeeded.

At his doctor's office on Grouse Creek, Robert often treated men hurt in the Grouse Creek War. The war had started early that spring when the owners of the Grouse Creek Bedrock Flume Company had come back from Victoria, where they had been raising money to buy hydraulic equipment, only to find the Canadian Company had taken over their claim. During their absence, the Canadian Company had applied for and been granted rights to the supposedly abandoned mine by the new Gold Commissioner. Bedrock Flume took their grievance to Miners Court and the court found in favor of the Bedrock

Flume company claim. A violent dispute erupted, and the local magistrate sent a message to Governor Joseph Seymour in New Westminster to send the marines. Seymour came himself and promised the men a new trial. During the interval, more vicious fights erupted and many of the Canadian Company men ended up in jail. The British Colonist reported on September 9, 1867, that the men spent "an agreeable time in jail as their friends supplied them with food and brew." The paper also reported that "they were the jolliest convicts ever seen."

However, there was a great deal happening behind the scene. Governor Seymour appointed Chartres Brew to replace Gold Commissioner Henry Maynard Ball and take charge of the Cariboo. He also appointed a Special Commissioner, Judge Joseph Needham, Vancouver Island's Chief Justice, to preside over the new trial which would be held in Barkerville. Needham's leisure time was often spent with Robert at his Grouse Creek cabin.

The trial was a test of the local justice system, which clearly upheld the rights of miners and the ownership of their claims. Evidence showed that the incompetent Gold Commissioner needed to be replaced (this had already been done) and the methods to settle disputed claims needed to be clarified. Robert wrote about all this in another letter to Sir John A. Macdonald and, without realizing it, he became a spokesman for the Cariboo. The verdict of the second trial was in favor of Bedrock Flume and peace finally returned to the Cariboo.

With winter approaching, many mines were closing. Barnard's Stages advertised in the *Cariboo Sentinel* that miners could travel to Yale in five days and Victoria in eight days. The Library, which had recently moved from Cameronton, requested that borrowed books be returned before October 10, 1867. Some miners, however, chose to stay to winter in the Cariboo. Both the Methodist and Anglican churches sponsored lectures during the winter months, and Rev. Reynard provided education classes for a fee. The Cariboo Dramatic Society, with Robert and his friends, staged several plays. The Masonic Lodge took on a benevolent program for destitute miners.

As the old year slipped into the new, Barkerville was gaining a sense of permanency. With many residents staying during the winter and many businesses remaining open, Barkerville was growing in stature and prosperity.

*The British Columbia parliament buildings, known as the "bird cages," under construction.*

*The main street of Barkerville at the height of the Cariboo gold rush.*

# 5. Elected Member of the British Columbia Legislature

With Barkerville's new growth and prosperity, Robert's medical practice flourished, as did his mining interests in two companies on Williams Creek and his two shares in the Minnehaha claim. His spare time was used constructively, reading political news and writing letters. One special letter was sent to his brother James Alexander, who had just been elected Mayor of Stratford, Ontario. Another letter, dated, February 21, 1868, was addressed to Sir John A. Macdonald:

> As chairman of a very large and influential meeting held here some weeks ago in this place, I take the liberty of forwarding you the paper containing the account of the proceedings and inviting your attention to the almost perfect unanimity of the Colonists in favor of the scheme of Confederation. That you are desirous of such a consummation from your recent speech sufficiently demonstrates that you fully appreciate the importance of such an acquisition to our common Canadian Dominion and I am at separation. I need not give you no time limit. You cannot however possibly be aware

of our great desire for its speedy accomplishment, but I can assure you of the fact. Being a Crown Colony, it is natural to refer that the official element would naturally be opposed to such a movement. It is thus that I account for ~~~~~of one government in making known to yours our ~~~~ formal wishes.

As a Canadian, I value your reputation ~~~~ properly ~~~~ in the smallest degree, or to mislead you, or to suffer you to be led, and I therefore hesitate that connection toward the population ~~~~in favor of immediate Confederation. May I beg you Sir John to give your earliest attention to this all import matter. And believe me to remain your most obedient and humble servant
R. W.W. Carrall
(~~~ is where words are not clear in document)

The doctor was shocked when the local newspaper reported that Honorable Thomas D'Arcy McGee had been assassinated on April 7, 1868. It was believed that McGee was killed by someone loyal to the Fenian cause. The Fenians were a radical group who wanted to take over Canada and use it as leverage to gain freedom for their countrymen in Ireland. Robert's own brother was in Saginaw, Michigan and was part of a group of Canadians willing to go to the border and fight for Canada.

With the report of McGee's assassination, Robert became worried about Sir John A. Macdonald's safety. In addition to the fear over the Fenians, Macdonald had to contend with the Riel Rebellion and a hostile Quebec faction. He was also busy with the formation of the Northwest Mounted Police.

In May, Amor De Cosmos, a member of the legislative council of British Columbia helped organize the Confederation League, the first body resembling a political party ever created in British Columbia. The League had two major goals, union with Canada and responsible government. Throughout the summer, the league staged a series of speeches to foster support for the union. Unfortunately, Governor Joseph Seymour opposed union with Canada.

In early June, Robert received a letter from Macdonald urging the young doctor to communicate with some of the leading men of the province. The Prime Minister also outlined some of his hopes and plans for the future. He saw Victoria as "a depot for the Northern Pacific, possibly a free port," which he said would "checkmate the importance of San Francisco and the Central Pacific Railroad." Macdonald also wrote that "the instant our union is completed, your cabinet (meaning the Dominion cabinet) should appropriate sufficient money for opening a thoroughfare from Fort William to Fort Gerry, from Fort Edmonton at the base of the Rocky Mountains and Barkerville in the Cariboo, which is 600 miles from Victoria." Macdonald also admits to Carrall that "although it was a utopian dream, a railroad across the country may be possible."

On July 1, 1868, Robert and J. S. Thompson were the main speakers at a largely- attended open-air meeting in Barkerville. Both men pointed out that contrary to a resolution passed in 1867 by the Legislative Council in favor of Confederation, the Council had later annulled the resolution, contending that a delay was necessary. At the meeting two resolutions were agreed upon: that the government of the Province opposed Confederation contrary to the wishes of the people, and the people should adopt an organized method of obtaining immediate admission into the Dominion. (*Critical Period of British Columbia* by the historian, Walter Sage)

Dr. Carrall had also organized a Queen Victoria's birthday celebration in the town with horse racing and fights being the main attractions. That same night, the young doctor was part of a cast in a play at Theater Royal for the miners' entertainment.

A few days later, there was an informal meeting between Robert, J. S. Thompson and H. E. Seelye in front of Scott Lipsett's Saloon. The three men decided to send a telegram to the Secretary of State in Ottawa outlining the resolutions that had been drafted regarding the confederation of the colony with the Dominion of Canada.

On August 4, 1868, Robert wrote another letter to Sir John A. Macdonald, advising him of the celebrations for Dominion Day. He also told the Prime Minister about the Confederation League. "The Head Centre is the Mayor of Victoria."

In addition to his political aspirations, Robert was still very busy with his medical practice. The *Colonist* reported that he had attended to a colored miner whose thumb had been severely injured when hoisting a gear in the mine. Unfortunately, despite Robert's efforts the man had to have the upper part of the joint amputated.

With the coming of fall to the Cariboo, herds of elk and moose could be seen silhouetted against the sky as they moved to lower feeding grounds. The nights were also cooler and morning frosts were the norm as the miners began to make preparations to head south for the winter.

On September 21st the aurora borealis, sometimes called the northern polar lights, put on a spectacular show. As a cold south wind swept down the canyon from Williams Creek, streamers of phosphorous green lights with faint red and purplish tones danced across the sky. The next morning a heavy frost etched the town in white.

However, by 3:00 on the afternoon of September 22, Barkerville was engulfed in flames. The fire was accidentally started by a zealous young man who tried to steal a kiss from a girl. In the skirmish, a stovepipe was accidentally knocked against the canvas roof of a room adjoining Barry and Adler's Saloon. The heat of the stove pipe immediately set the canvas ceiling on fire. Within seconds, sparks flew, igniting the roofs of nearby wooden buildings. The fire jumped across the street and moved from building to building. Explosions could be heard from inside the stores as coal oil cans and other inflammatory products exploded. One store owner put his dynamite and other wares down a mine shaft. Soon a roaring inferno was raging through the town

Men used water from the Barker flume in the center of the

town to douse the flames, but it only kept the fire at bay for a short time. People ran to their homes, businesses, and boarding houses to grab what they could, setting the items in the creek or in middle of the street. Robert's office, located over the Masonic Hall on the West side of street between Barnard Express Office and Strous's store, was soon ablaze and quickly burned to the ground. The contents were valued at $500. In less than three hours, the entire town was charred rubble.

That night people slept in the streets, shivering under a blanket or a coat, using whatever they could for a pillow. Robert and the other doctors in the area treated burns and cuts into the wee hours of the morning. Although the hospital, located considerable distance from Barkerville proper, was crowded with patients, there were no fatalities.

By dawn the next morning, help was on the way as local sawmills sent loads of lumber valued at an inflated $125 a thousand board feet. In the burned town, the miners combed through the debris, scraping away the ashes and clearing the mess so the town could rebuild. There was no time to waste as the winter cold was only weeks away and the men needed shelter.

While the fire contributed to the demise of Marysville, Cameron-ton and Richfield, it brought a new direction to Barkerville. Chartres Brew, the resident magistrate and Gold Commissioner, supervised the rebuilding of the pioneer town. He saw that the design of the buildings and boardwalks were improved, that the streets were widened and all safety requirements met. Three gas lights were installed, one in front of the bank and the other two strategically placed in the center of the town. Within days, although still in make-shift condition, Wake-up Jake's Café and bakeshop opened for business. Fanny Benndixon replaced her saloon with a more refined establishment, which featured a doorman at the entrance to welcome her clientele. The new Theater Royal opened with a greater seating capacity and soon had artists belting out songs like the Old Oaken Bucket and

Grenadier Guards. Dr Carrall was kept busy with his practice. Men fell off scaffolds, others strained their backs, broke limbs — the list of injuries was endless.

On October 14, 1868, a CARD was placed in the *Cariboo Sentinel*, addressed to Robt. W. W. Carrall, Esq., M.D.

Dear Sir: — We, the undersigned, electors of Cariboo, feeling the importance of having a representative from this district in the ensuring Legislative Council, who, while, understanding the wants of the mining community, is also prepared to strenuously advocate the grand despartum now required by this colony — viz., immediate Confederation with the Dominion of Canada — respectfully request you to allow yourself to be placed in nomination to-morrow.

The card was signed by 87 electors of the Cariboo. Carrall's reply was printed in the same issue of the *Cariboo Sentinel*. He said he was extremely pleased by the honor:

If elected, I may not succeed in accomplishing much in such a peculiar body as the Council now is, I shall do my best to carry out what reforms I can, and I hope you will all give advice in respect to what you consider could be done by your representative.

The meeting was held the next day at the Court House "with a highly respectable audience." Resident Magistrate C. Brew, Esq. announced that in accordance with instructions from the Governor he was prepared to receive nomination of candidates. Three were nominated, one declined, and when a show of hands favored Robert; the other man withdrew his name. When he got up to speak, Robert proclaimed that "this is the proudest moment of my life."

He then outlined four main issues which he said he would try to address in the Legislature:

- improvements and modifications to the mining laws;
- the excessive expenditures of the colony;
- a system of non-sectarian FREE school education; and
- expatriate the Confederation of British Columbia to the Dominion of Canada.

He ended his speech by saying that he would probably commit errors, but his heart was pure and his intentions were straightforward. Robert, the first elected legislator from the Cariboo, left Barkerville on November 14, 1868, for Victoria and the Legislative Council.

After the bone chilling cold of Barkerville, it was pleasurable to bask in the warm breezes of Victoria. It was also a pleasure to dine with old friends like Dr. Powell and share Christmas with him and his family. Robert was also able to go to Victoria's best tailor for new clothes: a dark morning coat with satin facing, dark trousers and high silk hat, and, of course, a fashionable colorful vest. He could well-afford the new wardrobe as his mining interests were paying off and he was able to add the Galer and Raby Companies to his portfolio.

Robert indulged himself further with his purchase of a velocipede, the forerunner of a bicycle and the first ever seen in the colony. However, he then had to learn to ride the two-wheeler. Unfortunately, he fell off many times, much to the amusement of his friends. (*The Mainland Guardian*, March 17, 1869)

In political circles, Robert voted against deeding Beacon Hill Park to Victoria, the colony's capital. He claimed that in the last 18 months, in which Victoria had been in charge of Beacon Hill Park, it had not expended a single dollar on it. Therefore, he felt Victoria was incompetent to administer the Park, the evidence being "the condition of the streets which were in a disgraceful condition." The Park was returned to the jurisdiction of the Legislative Council's Department of Lands and Works. (*Colonist*, March 5, 1869)

Earlier in the new year, the Hon. Dr. Carrall received a congratulatory letter from Sir John A. Macdonald. The Prime Minister said he liked Robert's suggestion that several prominent government men visit the province. Another letter, dated April 28, 1869, came from Ottawa addressed to R.W.W. Carrall, Esq. M.P.P., Barkerville, British Columbia:

I am in receipt of your very interesting letter of the 2nd April as to the state of feeling in British Columbia and Vancouver Island. I have given it to Sir John Young, our Governor General, for his perusal.

You will have heard, ~~~ this, of the great progress of events with respect to the Hudson's Bay Territory. The British Government have succeeded in forcing the Company to transfer the sovereignty and proprietorship of the Country to the Dominion of Canada, on reasonable terms, and we are now in daily expectation of receiving the official despatch from the Colonial Office, informing us of the transfer. We shall then proceed at once to take a vote of our Parliament here on the question. I have no doubt that the terms will be accepted by our Legislature.

We shall then, without delay, apply for the proclamation from Her Majesty, adding the Country to the Dominion of Canada under the terms of the Confederation Act. Newfoundland will, I believe, also become a portion of our union, and then we only wait for you to embrace all British North America.

I have no doubt that Lord Granville will take immediate steps in the way of instructing your Governor to press the subject on the consideration of your Legislature.

Believe me
My dear Sir
Sincerely yours,
John a. Macdonald

*Dr Carrall's office at Barkerville.*

# 6. Champion of the Interior

There were still several impediments to British Columbia's union with Canada, including the increased momentum of the American annexation movement, which had begun 1867, and a worsening economic recession.

Well aware that Governor Joseph Seymour was against Confederation, journalist Henry E. Seelye, a strong supporter of Robert and Confederation, wrote to Sir John A. Macdonald asking for the recall of Governor Seymour. However, Macdonald had already suggested to Governor General Young that he transfer Anthony Musgrave, Governor of Newfoundland to British Columbia. It was a well known fact that Musgrave was very much in favor of Confederation as he had tried unsuccessfully to have Newfoundland become part of the Dominion of Canada.

At the close of the spring session of the Legislature, Robert returned to the Cariboo, where he still retained his medical practice. In June, he attended to Alfred Dow, a miner, who was caught in a cave-in at the Waverley tunnel at Grouse Creek. Dow had badly injured his face, neck, and right hand. Robert was also called upon to be a juror in a Supreme Court case at the Richfield Court House. He also attended his mining interest in the Minnehaha claim on Harvey Creek, and took part in a play at the Theater Royal.

On June 24, 1869, he was involved in the consecration of the new and spacious Cariboo Lodge, the new home of the Masons. That evening the members celebrated the festival of St. John the Baptist. Wake-up-Jake's Restaurant catered to the banquet, at which Robert, like many of the others, drank and ate more than he should.

Meanwhile, the young politician was busy organizing a gala celebration for Dominion Day, to which a number of the citizens had voluntarily subscribed funds. In mid-June a meeting was held at the theater and a program for the day was adopted. Instead of giving away prize money for the horse races, it was proposed that a silver plate and cup be given designated as the Queen's Plate and the Dominion Cup. Some of the wealthier citizens of the Cariboo had brought in good racing stock from San Francisco. Something new had been added to the celebration that year — a velocipede race. Following Robert's example, several of these big front wheel bicycles, had been purchased by other daring citizens of Barkerville.

Robert suspected another gold rush was in the making as gold had been discovered in the Omineca region of the interior at Vital and Germansen Creeks. Many miners from Barkerville were heading north to the almost inaccessible region and others were expected from the Washington Territory and California. In addition to mining, the Omineca plateau offered good grazing land for cattle, and several ranches were already operating. Robert realized that people going to the Omineca were going to need supplies and to transport these supplies a good road was needed. At the time, the only ways into the Omineca region of the northern interior were water routes: Fort St. James from Tache and Stuart Rivers; the Baldy Mountain route; and the Hazleton and Skeena River route. The fourth route ran up the Fraser River over Giscome Portage to Summit Lake through to McLeod Lake and up the Finley and Omineca Rivers. These were long arduous routes, and the cost of shipping supplies was extremely high.

During the next few months, Robert met with important men in British Columbia, pioneers like F. J. Bernard who had carried mail on foot to the miners in the Cariboo before developing his own stage line, Legislators C. F. Cornwall from Yale, R. J. Skinner from Kootenay, Hugh Nelson, the member for New Westminster, and G. B. Wright. These men drafted the "Memorial in Connection with the Omineca Road" petition and addressed it to His Excellency, Governor Musgrave of the Legislative Council of British Columbia

The petition read:

The undersigned have been requested by the people of British Columbia to present, in connection with the Omineca Road Petition, the Memorial entering more of the details regarding the object for necessity of the said Petition.

It is now exceedingly probable that several hundred miners are going to the new mine in the Omineca District very early in the ensuing spring Unless new developments are made in the Cariboo, it will be deprived of at least ½ of the present population.

In the agricultural district every man who is able to leave his farming interest is intending to go in the same direction.

We can reasonable calculate 3 or 400 from Victoria, Washington Territory and California; it is not an exaggerated estimate to believe that 1200 or 1500 men in a short time will be en route to Germansen Creek. A great many of them will strive to reach the mines as soon as the weather will allow them to travel and before it is possible to transport food or mining tools over the present route.

It follows, therefore, that there will be an inevitable delay at some point in their journey, unless additional facilities are provided for them to reach their destination. In such a case great suffering might ensure and a reaction would probably take place which would retard the prospecting of the country.

To avoid this there is one route capable of affording early relief. This is the route proposed to be opened from Quesnelmouth via Giscome Portage. The ordinary time at which ice disappears from the Upper Fraser River and the water leading to and from Lake Macleod is April 20th. Upon Tala Lake, it invariable remains about a month later, often not breaking up until June. Even after the ice is gone from the lake, the grass upon the trail from Tala Landing to Omineca River is insufficient to support the animals until nearly July 1. Thus the Fraser River will allow transportation of supplies about 6 weeks earlier than the one hitherto followed.

This route has another advantage over others. In event of it being opened a larger number of boats will be at once constructed at Quesnelmouth, and each miner who has the money to get his summer's supplies will be able to land them directly in the heart of the mines. The boats will give them ready means of moving them up or down the river and their prospecting will be made a matter of little difficulty. If, however, men are compelled to carry their food upon their backs through forests without trails, their efforts will be limited to a very few creeks.

It is supposed that Germans Creek does not lie more than 110 miles from the Giscome Portage. Through this section of the country there are many chains of lakes surrounded by good grass through which a trail could easily be opened. By that trail the principal portion of the foot travel would eventfully pass.

Besides the interest of the mining population it seems to be necessary to protect the interests of the farmers. During the past season, the Talloes, Thompson, Kamloops, Bonaparte and Soda Creek Districts have produced more than 3,000,000 bushels of wheat This when ground would yield 1,000 tons of flour, an amount double the requirements of the entire mining and farming population. If half of the Cariboo should leave for the Northern mines, the surplus of flour will be very large and the producers will be unable to dispose of their produce at any except ruinous rates. If no outlet for this produce is provided for the Cariboo market, it is thought that ½ of the land under cultivation will not be farmed during the ensuing season.

As evident of the low prices which farmers are now getting for grain, we will state that wheat is being bought to Kamloops Lake already sacked after being transported 40 miles for 1 3/4 cents per lb. — a trifle only above the price in San Francisco. The same remarks apply to other produce and to cattle, hogs and sheep.

The entire mercantile Community of British Columbia are closely connected with the farming population and their interests are identical. The barter and the credit systems prevail throughout the whole country. If, therefore, the latter class are deprived of a portion of their market, a universal depression will exist among the traders, and many of them will be ruined. Such a result could not fail to seriously injure Victoria and other principal towns.

The amount that is asked from the Government for the proposed roads and trails is small. A few individuals from one single thinly populated district have contributed upwards of Five Thousand Dollars for the explorations which have already been made. Only six times this amount is asked from the whole country. If, by means of this small outlay one thousand men should be enabled to remain in the Omineca country for the space of one year, the amount expended by the Government would be received back, or nearly so, in Customs Duties and Tolls on the merchandise consumed by them. In this event, the Government would in that space of time actually be reimbursed for its expenditure.

It is evident at the influx of a large mining population, and the full development of the extensive gold field which undoubtedly exists upon the Peace River and its tributaries will give the Colony an additional importance in the eyes of the people of Canada. As a means of bartering Confederation, and of securing the most favorable terms of Union, it, therefore seems to be the true policy of the Government to render that country easy of access.

In regard to the feasibility of the scheme of opening this route, and the time which will be consumed in carrying goods over it, we beg to append the following statement from well-known miners:–

"Peace River Smith" was two days going from the Giscome Portage to Macleod's Lake, and two more from there to Findlay's River:

"Black Jack" was five days going from Findlay's River to Germans Creek, and poled his canoe the whole distance:

John Giscome says he could go from Germans Creek to the Portage in seven days in a canoe, or either way in twelve days with loaded boats:

"Nick Silver" made the trip from the mouth of Nation River up to Macleod's Lake in a dug out in 3 ½ days. "I think the trail north from Macleod's Lake would be through very thinly timbered country, small cottonwoods and Black pine, with good grace."

"Dancing Bill" says "I can go from Portage to Findlay's Branch in four days. Have been up Parsnip River 40 miles above Macleod's River. It is good for steam boating: plenty of water and not rapid. I think it is not over 75 miles from Macleod's Lake to the head of Germans Creek."

All the above believe that a good and easy trail could be opened almost in a direct line from Macleod's Lake to Germans Creek.

In conclusion we wish to state to your Excellency — That responsible boatmen have expressed a willingness to freight from Quesnelmouth to Germans Creek (provided the road across the Portage is opened) for 10 cents per lb. And think that when the route is fairly tested this can be reduced. Freight from Quesnel to Tatlah Landing during the last season cost 12 ½ cents

R.W.W. Carrall, Member for Cariboo

C.F. Cornwall, Member for Yale
R. J. Skinner, Member for Kootenay
Hugh Nelson, Member for New Westminster
F.J. Barnard,
G.B. Wright
(Courtesy of Bancroft Library)

This was an impressive document, but it would be two years before a road, using the Fraser River route, would be built by Gustavus Blin. This Memorial in Connection with the Omineca Road Petition became one of the most important documents drafted by Dr. Carrall.

The new year of 1870 began with Robert's appointment as an unofficial member of the Executive Council of British Columbia Legislature. This allowed him and fellow appointee Dr. John Sebastian Helmcken to take part in framing the terms of union, which, if accepted by the Colony of British Columbia's Legislative Council, would then be submitted to Ottawa for their consideration. Then, if accepted by the government of Canada, it would result in the colony's admission to Confederation.

The Executive Council was made up of His Excellency Governor A. Musgrave and the following Honorable members: the Colonial Secretary, the Attorney General, the Chief Commissioner of Lands and Works and the Collector of Customs, who were now joined by J. S. Helmcken and R. W. W. Carrall.

Over the next few weeks the Council hammered out 16 terms that they felt were necessary if the Colony was to become part of Canada. The most important term was that "Canada shall be liable for the debts, and liabilities of British Columbia existing at the time of the Union," as recorded in the minutes of the Executive Council, February 9, 1870. It was no secret that the colony was in financial difficulties.

In March 1870, the Great Confederation Debates began in the Legislative Council. As the debates continued day after day, voices grew louder and tempers flared. Some felt that British Columbia would be overwhelmed by a central government. Others feared for their jobs and pension if the Colony joined Confederation. A few argued that the Dominion Government could not be trusted and questioned the integrity of the Dominion government and its officials. By March 17, Robert had heard enough and jumped to his feet. He could hold his temper no longer:

> I have sat in this Council for two sessions, and have endeavored to conduct myself with propriety, but I find certain Hon. Gentlemen in this Council who by innuendo and implication, directly and indirectly, have endeavored to cast slurs upon Canada, and to slander and belittle the Statesmen of that Country which I am proud to call my own ... because my country occupies too high a place in the roll of England's Colonies to be affect by such conduct ... For my part, I look upon the Queen's proclamation as the guarantee which will make the whole thing inviolable.

Later, in that same speech, Robert said that he was against Responsible Government at this time: "Once we are in the Dominion, and if the people desire it, no power on earth can prevent them from having it." As a result, he was severely criticized by certain members of the Legislative and blasted in the presses for this statement. However, the following day he explained his reasons for being against Responsible Government at this particular time:

> It is perfectly clear to all that as soon as we enter the Confederacy, the people of this country can have any form of government they desire ... I am equally aware of the priceless boon of responsibility which exists in England, which may be called the Standard-Bearer of the nation, and I am equally aware that the same responsibility does not exist in United States. During the late war I was in the United States army. Stanton, then the Secretary of War, was a most

unpopular man. They wanted to get rid of him, but he could not be removed.

When I took the ground that responsible government was not expedient, it was not because I did not approve of the system. It is, I say, the wisest and best form of government, but it is too cumbrous for this colony. The Council contains no men of influence, the constituencies are too remote and the inhabitants are all engaged in bread-seeking; there are few men of independent means who would take part in responsible government and consequently the direction of public affairs would fall into the hands of men who are not fitted or qualified to govern the country.

Finally, after weeks of arguing the resolutions that the Executive Council had recommended were accepted as the terms of union that would be put before the Dominion government. Governor Anthony Musgrave then chose three men to take "the terms of union" to Ottawa. He chose Chief Commissioner of Lands and Works, Joseph William Trutch, Victoria City's elected member of the Legislature Council, Dr. John Sebastian Helmcken, and Dr. Robert William Weir Carrall, the elected representative of the Cariboo. Each man had his own particular area of expertise. Governor Musgrave said, "Dr. Carrall is a Canadian and a zealous advocate of union who is interested in political power, not for himself, but for the country." Then, he added that Carrall "is familiar with the wants and view of the people of the Upper Country and he will be able to render service in explaining these to the Canadian Government."

While the delegates were preparing to go to Ottawa, there was a lot happening in the Dominion. On April 6, the British Minister at Washington had alerted Ottawa of projected Fenian raids along the Canada-American frontier from St. Albans to Port Huron. These raids took on a personal tone when Robert learned in a letter from home that his brother, who lived in Saginaw, Michigan, was involved in forming a Canadian contingent to fight the Fenians at the Port Huron border. Just as distressing was word in the newspapers that Sir John A. Macdonald was absent from the House of Commons due to illness.

Problems were developing on the home front too as local school boards needed more money to keep their schools open. To raise extra funds, the Executive Council wanted the Legislature to impose an additional tax of half a dollar on a gallon of spirits. This would supersede a bill already sent to the Legislature, April 29, 1870. The Council also wanted Joseph Trutch, the Chief Commissioner of Lands and Works, to arrange for their agent with the telegraph system in Washington Territory to come to Victoria to complete arrangements for the transfer of the telegraph line from Victoria to the Cariboo to the government of British Columbia.

On May 10, the three delegates, Trutch, Helmcken, and Carrall, left Victoria for San Francisco on the steamboat *Active* en route to Ottawa. They were accompanied by Mrs. Trutch and H. E. Seelye, special correspondent for the *Daily British Colonist*. Each delegate was allowed $1,000 for expenses.

*Miners posed at the Minnhehaha mine, partly owned by Dr Carrall.*

# 7. The Road to Union with the Dominion

Since there was no direct link between Ottawa and British Columbia, the delegates had to travel by boat to San Francisco and then by train eastward. However, they were able to get a first-hand view of the railroad that had been built through the mountains over terrain similar to that of British Columbia. As they traveled east and northward to Canada, they were also impressed with the bridges, especially those that spanned the Mississippi River.

At Buffalo, the delegates parted company with Carrall and Helmcken traveling to Woodstock and the Trutches and Seelye going on to Kingston and Ottawa. Robert was anxious to see his father, Sheriff James Carrall, who was nearing 80 and whom he hadn't seen in several years.

Woodstock had planned a gala homecoming for Robert, and Dr. Helmcken was asked to attend. That night about 150 people heard Dr. Helmcken praise Robert's work in the Cariboo. Helmcken also talked very frankly about Confederation and British Columbia's desire to be part of the Dominion, stressing the fact that the railway would only cost taxpayers a $1 a head. (*Globe*, June 10, 1870)

> With us, Union is not a sentiment. We have lived and prospered in our isolated position and will continue to do so unless by union we can do something for the future of British Columbia ...union is a necessity for us. British Columbia is not a poor country ... but I may as well tell you in all candor that, while I am disposed to accept Confederation, I accept it, and the people of British Columbia will accept it, but on this condition — that through the exertions of the people of the Dominion a railway from the Atlantic to the Pacific is the result. Let us not deceive ourselves. You have a far West, to which a railroad is a necessity. We also have an untold wealth, which a railway will develop. Why not unite our energies and construct a railway for the benefit of both, and by the agency of which a nation may be given, will make this Continent more powerful than England herself? The Americans now have a Pacific railway, and in a short time this will be supplemented by a Northern and a Southern Pacific railway, and the railway by which we have reached this place came a thousand miles over an arid plain.

That night Robert was given another honor when the Masons of Oxford Lodge #76 presented him with a life membership. Leaving Woodstock the next day, the two doctors took a side trip to Niagara Falls.

Carrall and Helmcken arrived in Ottawa on Friday, June 3, 1870. When the government was notified of their arrival, the delegates received a message from Sir John Young, the Governor-General of Canada, asking them to meet him at 3:00 o'clock in his office in the parliament buildings. Shortly afterward, Young was joined by Sir George Cartier, the Minister of Militia and Defence and the Acting Prime Minister, who then escorted them to the Privy Council Chambers, where they met Hon. Joseph Howe and several of the Privy Council members.

That night, the delegates, Mrs. Trutch and H. E. Seelye, were entertained at dinner by Hon. Joseph Howe, Hon. Mr. Tilley, Minister of Customs, and Sir Francis Hicks, Minister of Finance. Robert had met Sir Francis Hincks many years ago when the minister had run against Peter Carrall, his uncle, in an election for a seat in the Upper Canada Legislature. Peter lost the election.

When Robert learned of the seriousness of Sir John's illness, he immediately sent a letter of sympathy to the Prime Minister. He was surprised when a message came back that Sir John wanted to see him. Although the two men had corresponded, they had never previously met. When Joseph Trutch found out that the young doctor was going to see the Prime Minister, he was put out. He felt that if any of the delegates were to see the ailing Prime Minister, it should have been he.

For his meeting with the Prime Minister, Robert dressed very carefully. He wore a tailed morning coat, a white starched shirt, and a moderately subdued cravat. Instead of arranging for a carriage, he decided to walk the short distance to the East Block of the parliament buildings, where Macdonald's office had been turned into accommodation for the Prime Minister when he had been stricken with a gallstone attack in the House. Carrall was so excited about his visit with the Prime Minister that he didn't even notice the smoke-tinged air from the numerous forest fires burning north east of the capital.

Agnes Macdonald greeted Robert, looking stern in her dark high-necked dress. She told the young doctor in no uncertain terms that he was *not* to upset her husband, who, unfortunately was still suffering from a severe attack of gallstones. However, a light smile broke the severity of her words when she acknowledged that against her advice and that of his doctor, Sir John A. was determined to meet the young man from British Columbia who had dreams similar to his own for Canada.

Macdonald, sitting in a lounging-type chair with a carpet wrapped around his legs, immediately held out his frail hand to Robert. As the two men shook hands, there was no doubt in Robert's mind that the Prime Minister had been very close to death. Soon after their initial greetings were over, Sir John asked, "Have you got your conditions all right?" (*Victoria Daily Standard*, December 6, 1873). Carrall said he was well prepared for the forthcoming meetings. Far too soon Agnes Macdonald touched Robert's shoulder, and he knew it was time to leave. But the two men would meet again; of that, Robert was sure.

On Monday, June 6, 1870 the three men went directly to the Acting Prime Minister's office, where they found Sir George Cartier in his shirt sleeves already hard at work. Shrugging into his jacket, Cartier apologized and offered them a glass of sherry. The Acting Prime Minister's office, although cooler (the temperature outside was 90 degrees in the shade) was quite different from any offices Carrall had ever seen with its designed carpet, gold-beige walls and Venetian-type blinds that shut out the western sun. As soon as the men finished their drinks, Cartier escorted them to the Privy Council chambers, where preliminary matters were to be discussed. The main function of the Privy Council, which had been established under the Constitution Act of 1867, was to study constitutional matters and advise the government. It was in these chambers that the terms of union would be accepted, rejected, or modified.

On June 7, 1870, it was all business when the delegates again met in the Privy Council chambers with Sir George Etienne Cartier, Sir Frances Hincks, and the Hon. Mr. Tilley. Mr. Trutch occupied the Governor General's seat with Helmcken on his right and Robert on his left. It was an accepted fact that Joseph Trutch would head the delegation. (Helmcken Diaries). The general terms of union were discussed for about three hours. Afterwards, Helmcken and Sir Francis Hincks discussed tariffs, Trutch discussed legalities, and Robert talked about the interior of British Columbia. He told the minister about BC's resources, including gold, silver, lumber, and coal. He also said that just today he had received word that the first salmon fish cannery had been opened on the Fraser River.

Tariffs became a stumbling block for Sir Francis Hincks until Sir George Cartier conceived the brilliant idea of British Columbia giving up land for the railway and the government compensating the colony. The meeting ended on a jovial note when the delegates learned that they were to dine that evening with Governor General Sir John Young and Lieutenant-Colonel Chamberlain.

On June 8, 1870, it was agreed that Canada would be liable for British Columbia's debts at time of union, and that the population, for the purposes of financial arrangements, would be placed at 120,000, certainly less than it actually was. The delegates also discussed a first-class graving dock at Esquimalt. Later that day, they were pleasantly surprised with the news that they were invited to go to Montreal for the investiture of Prince Arthur, the third son of Queen Victoria. Afterward, they would travel to Quebec to see the Presentation of Colors to the 68th Regiment and their consecration. The delegates realized they would be absent for a week, but they were determined to utilize their time in discussing the business of union with various members of the parliament who would be on the train through to Quebec.

On June 11, 1870, at Montreal the delegates attended the investiture of Prince Arthur at St. Patrick's Hall by Governor General Sir John Young. At the ceremonies, they had a perfect view as they were seated among the Cabinet ministers. Later at an afternoon reception, Prince Arthur assured them that as soon as a railroad was completed over British soil, he would visit British Columbia. That evening Mr. Trutch dined privately with the Prince. (*Gazetteer*, June 11, 1870)

The next morning on the train to Quebec City, the delegates again used their time constructively as they talked one-on-one to members of the government about some of the significant points of union and what it could mean to the people of British

Columbia. Robert, of course, was at his best describing the benefits that the interior of the colony offered in Canada.

The Presentation of Colors by Prince Arthur to the 68th Regiment at Quebec was a brilliant affair with the crowds, all in colorful holiday attire, numbering in the thousands. The part of the Esplanade selected for the ceremony was a hollow bastion at the lower end of the Citadel. The 69th Regiment, very colorful in their blue peaked caps, blue pants, and dark blue tunics, arrived on the grounds at 11:00 a.m. and were drawn up in a line facing westward.

A 19-gun salute from the Citadel announced the approach of the royal cortege from Spencerwood, the home of the Lieutenant-Governor of Quebec, where the Prince and his entourage had spent the night. A few minutes later, the carriages carrying the Governor-General, Prince Arthur, and the Lieutenant-Governor arrived on the grounds. The BC delegates again had some of the best seats as they sat with the Members of the Legislature. Robert was surprised to hear that the 69th Regiment had served on a ship with Nelson at Trafalgar, been in hostilities at Java, and had been in India during the mutiny. In his speech, Prince Arthur also pointed out that the regiment "with efficiency and discipline on May 28, 1870, had taken several Fenian prisoners." (*Globe*, June 21, 1870)

On June 24, 1870, Sir Francis Hicks, the Minister of Finance, sponsored an informal dinner and entertainment for H. E. Seelye, the *Daily British Colonist* correspondent who had accompanied the delegation to Ottawa.

On June 25, 1879, it was back to the negotiating table with the delegates often conferring with Governor Musgrave in Victoria by telegraph. Helmcken was absent from the talks as he had gone to New York for a few days.

On June 27, 1870, the Dominion government agreed to build a dry dock at Esquimalt and a marine hospital at Victoria, which would admit other patients upon making reasonable allowance.

Pensions were to be given to executive officials of the Colony whose services were terminated because of Confederation. However, the most import clause in the treaty provided for the construction of a railway to connect the seaboard of British Columbia with the railway system of eastern Canada.

The delegates from British Columbia also requested that the terms of union agreement be kept secret until they were presented to Governor Musgrave. Then, after the documents were formally signed by the Governor-General, the documents were entrusted to Robert to personally deliver them to Governor Musgrave in Victoria.

*Dr Helmcken and Dr Carroll discussing the politics involved in leading British Columbia into the Dominion of Canada.*

*Niagara Falls at the time Dr Helmcken and Dr Carrall visited the site.*

# 8. Senator Carrall

Robert Carrall arrived back in British Columbia on September 24, 1870. After a satisfactory meeting with Governor Musgrave, he was later disturbed to learn that the public schools were closed due to lack of money and children had to be educated at home. He had always been an advocate of a free public school education for all children.

It was then back to the Cariboo, where, within a couple of weeks, Robert was caught up in another election. On October 15, 1870, he was again nominated for the District of the Cariboo, but this time he had a worthy opponent in C. Booth, who was the favored representative in the areas of Keithly and Soda Creek.

While politicking throughout Barkerville and the surrounding area, he learned that the only gold mines making money were at Lightning Creek, where companies had invested in machinery sufficiently powerful to contend with their chief difficulty — water. He also learned that more miners were going to Omineca.

Robert's platform during this election campaign was much the same as it had been two years ago: mining laws needed to be reformed, the tariffs on 'laying over' were too high, and every child had a right to free education. The qualifications for voters were the following:

Voters had to be male of 21 years,
natural born British subject, or able to read English
and a resident of the district for at least 3 months.

When the final results were tallied on November 19, 1870, Robert won Barkerville, Van Winkle and Keithly, and C. Booth was successful at Quesnel and Soda Creek. A total of 590 votes were cast with Robert receiving a plurality of 307 votes. *The Mainland Guardian*, November 16, 1879, would later report that "the contest for the Cariboo district has resulted in a victory for the previous representative. The struggle was carried on with great determination, in perfect good humor between the friends of the rival candidates. Although there was plenty of chaff — and a large sum of money changed hands on the event — there was no breach of the peace."

On December 17, 1870, Robert left Barkerville for the Legislature. The weather was cold and clear with two to three feet of snow on the divide. So with a muffler around his neck, a hot brick at his feet, and a buffalo robe over his lap, he left for Quesnelmouth in a sleigh owned by Mr. Barlow and driven by Mr Work. From there, it was on to Yale, where he spent Christmas drinking current wine, a harmless beverage of the holidays. When he boarded the steamer at Alexander, just below Yale, there was ice on the Fraser River, which made the trip very hazardous. Although he would laugh about it later, Robert was very shaken by the experience: "I never passed so much time on my knees as I did coming down the Fraser on the steamer," he said. (*New Westminster Mainland Guardian*, January 19, 1871).

Robert was elated when he received a letter dated January 10, 1871, from Sir John A. Macdonald. The Prime Minister stated that the conditions of union were so satisfactory that not a single vote was cast against it in the House of Commons. Macdonald also said, "you might honor us with a visit this summer, just to cement the union." He then added, "I assure you many people respect you and would welcome you.". On January 20, 1871, the terms of union were accepted unanimously by the Legislature of British Columbia.

In other business in the Legislature, Robert supported a motion for the survey of a trail from Shuswap via Eagle Pass to Wild Horse Creek. He felt that a road would enable British Columbia traders to compete with those from the American side for the Kootenay trade. He said the Government of Lands and Works Department was negligent because this work should have been done long ago.

During the February session, Carrall asked leave to introduce a bill to facilitate the introduction of the Thomson Patent Road Steamers to the colony. He emphasized the importance of encouraging the introduction of machinery and the employing of foreign capital in the development of mineral wealth of the colony. These road steamers, of course, would supplement the mule trains by hauling freight. Unfortunately, time proved that the steamers, which resembled steam rollers, were adequate on the straightaways but were thwarted by precipitously steep grades like those at Jackass Mountain.

Robert also felt that there were good men in the colony who would run for office if the qualifications of real and personal property were lowered. He voted for an amendment reducing the lease hold qualifications of voters from $40 to $20 and proposed that a clause be added to alter qualifications of members fixing it at $1,500 real and $2,000 personal property.

On March 10, 1871, aware of the colony's depleted coiffures, Robert brought to the floor of the house a bill that would reduce the salary of the Chief Commissioner of the Land and Works Department, whom he felt was not doing his job. He also advocated that the salaries of other heads of departments be reduced. "We need to chop off the dead branches," he said. The bill was defeated seven to six. (*New Westminster Mainland* , April 1, 1871)

It wasn't all politics and pleasure for Robert. He, also, took time out from his legislature duties to attend the funeral of a Masonic member in New Westminster. It was an impressive ceremony, as reported in the *Mainland*. "A firing party took up their positions and fired the customary volleys over the grave of the departed officer."

From his Ottawa correspondence, Robert learned that the Uniform Currency Act, proposed by Sir Francis Hincks, was being debated in the House of Commons. If accepted, it would provide a common currency backed by government bonds and put the Bank of Montreal in the position of a central bank, thus changing the nature of banking in Canada. Robert, in particular, was interested in a strong banking system as he was now a wealthy man thanks to his shares in the Minnehaha and other claims.

By mid-July, he was back in Barkerville to celebrate the birth of the Province of British Columbia and its admittance to the Dominion of Canada. At midnight on July 19, 1871, bells rang, whistles blew and drinks flowed "We now have a flag of our own," Robert said as he happily saluted their new red, white and blue flag. Glasses were again raised when artist W. W. Hill presented Robert with his painting of the Union Jack, which he had dedicated to the young doctor.

In Victoria, the province's capital, crowds also gathered to celebrate the admission of British Columbia to the Dominion of Canada. At the nearby port of Esquimalt, a 21-gun salute was fired by the flagship *Zealous*. But not everyone was happy. Some feared for their jobs and others lamented that the province would now take orders from Ottawa.

On July 29, 1871, Robert left for Quesnelmouth, Omineca, and the northern interior of British Columbia. Omineca, the native word for slow-moving water, was a beautiful unexplored area with mountains, plateaus, and dozens of unnamed rivers, lakes and creeks. He followed the petition route via the Giscome

Portage and Tala Lake and, even with the construction of the new road, traveling was difficult. Since accommodation was almost nonexistent, he sometimes stayed overnight at the homestead of a rancher or at an isolated miner's camp. More often than not, however, he slept out in the open on the bank of an unnamed creek that was usually haunted by clouds of mosquitoes.

Along the way, he saw firsthand settlements springing to life as numerous sawmills turned out lumber for everything from sluice boxes to cabins. By mid-August, Robert had reached the settlement at Manson Creek, where several prospectors had already found gold. Then it was on to Germansen, a typical mining camp with makeshift stores and saloons.

He also heard about the many hardships of 1870. Miners told him they couldn't even buy a shovel or pick and that food was so expensive some almost starved during the winter. Mail, too, was haphazard, often delivered that winter by dog sled — and was costly too at $2.50 a letter. Fortunately, the Omineca Express was now able to connect with Barnard's Express and Wells Fargo to deliver mail and parcels to and from New Westminster and Victoria. Despite these inconveniences, if a miner was lucky, he could become a rich man.

Since Robert had been in Victoria in May and June, he knew that changes were coming to the Omineca. Peter O'Reilly, the Gold Commission and tax collector, the only government man in the district, was being replaced by W. H. Fitzgerald, who intended to build a residence at nearby Dunkeld. Robert also told the locals about trade with the Americans and British Columbia's terms of union with the Dominion of Canada.

Because there were no doctors in the area, he was often asked to set or reset broken bones, treat numerous infections, and offer advice. With his knowledge of botany, he was able to show the miners what wild plants could be used for medicinal purposes and food.

As he traveled westward, Robert met up with Jean Jacques

Caux, better known to the miners as Cataline, a mule freight packer who for years had delivered supplies to the Omineca. Cateline did not have formal schooling but was able to keep accurate records thanks to his remarkable memory. It was he who probably told Carrall about the Hagwilget Bridge. On his way west to Hazleton and the Skeena River, Robert detoured north to see the Hagwilget Canyon and the 150-feet long, 6-feet wide suspension bridge over the Bulkley River. Built on the cantilever principle by the indigenous population, whose only tools were knives and axes, the bridge was constructed of tree trunks, counter-weighted with logs and boulders. The planking was lashed to the frame with cedar ropes, as were the logs that spanned the gap between the two sides.

Unexpectedly, Robert came upon abandoned telegraph poles and supplies, which were expected to connect the American West to Russian territories in Siberia. Although the line already stretched from Quesnel to Hagwilget, where it crossed the Buckley River to the village of Kisplox and the Fort Stager station, Western Union had cancelled the project when a competitor made the line financially unfeasible.

While he was away in Omineca, Robert's future was being shaped by Sir John A. Macdonald, who had sent Hon. H. Langevin, Minister of Public Works to British Columbia, to find out who best should represent the province in the Senate of Canada. There would be three senators, two senators for the mainland and one for the island. Robert's name was on the short-list as a senator for the mainland.

The qualifications for senatorship were laid out specifically in the British North America Act (BNA) of 1867:

1. He shall be of the full age of thirty years.
2. He shall be either a natural born subject, or naturalized by Act of Parliament or Legislature, or of the parliament after the union.

3. He must own land within the province of which he is appointed, valued at $4000.
4. His real and personal property shall be together worth $4000 over his debts and liabilities.
5. He shall be a resident in the Province for which he is nominated.

The British North America Act also stated that senators could hold their seat for life, or until they resigned, and it was the responsibility of the Governor-General to summon qualified persons to the Senate.

Langevin discussed the senatorships at length with Joseph Trutch, the new Lieutenant-Governor of the province. Trutch said he believed that John Sebastian Helmcken was the best man to represent the island, but he felt that Ottawa had to make the senatorship financially attractive to Helmcken as he had a motherless family to support. Trutch also told Langevin that Robert Carrall and Clement Frances Cornwall, a barrister and a Conservative who lived about 80 miles from Yale, were the best men for the mainland.

In a letter to Sir John A., dated August 21, 1871, Langevin wrote that Dr. Carrall "does not wish to go into politics again. He is under the impression that the Ottawa government would be disposed to do something for him on account of his share in the confederation arrangement." Nevertheless, at the Police Barracks in Victoria, on October 14, 1871, Messrs. Helmcken, Cornwall, and Carrall were appointed to the three senator positions from the new province of British Columbia.

Robert left for the East on December 23, 1871. He had written his brother Henry that he would be able to celebrate the New Year at the family home in Oxford County, the same home where he had been born 32 years ago. He had only been in Woodstock a few days when he received some private correspondence from Sir John A. Macdonald, dated January 1872:

I telegraphed you, congratulating you on your safe arrival from parts unknown. It is not yet settled as when Parliament will meet, but you, of course, will get early notice. I propose going to Toronto next week, and if you have nothing to do, you might come down to `---- -------    Queen's Hotel.

Robert did visit the Prime Minister at the Queen's Hotel in Toronto before traveling on to Ottawa, where the young bachelor soon became the darling of the Ottawa social set as he was young, personable, and very rich.

*Dr Carrall's official Senate portrait.*

# 9. The Red Chamber

The year 1872 was an eventful one for Robert Carrall. He spent several days in early January with Sir John A. Macdonald, Agnes Macdonald and their son Hugh at the Queen's Hotel in Toronto. He and Sir John discussed everything from Robert's role as a senator to the election that was coming before the end of the year. It would be a difficult campaign, Sir John said, as many in French-Canada felt that he had treated Louis Riel with extreme severity. Others, especially in Ontario, had felt he had been too lenient. There was a problem with the railways as two powerful men wanted to be president of the Canadian Pacific Railway, Sir Hugh Allan of Montreal and David Macpherson of Toronto. Sir John said that he would need Robert's astute and sobering second thoughts on these matters in the Senate.

Robert arrived in Ottawa in mid-January. After getting settled in his room at the Russell House, he walked to the parliament buildings. He wanted to see the Senate Chamber on his own, sit at one of the desks, and feel its historic ambience. The Senate, sometimes called the Red Chamber, was patterned after the British House of Lords, where one of Robert's ancestors had sat more than 100 years ago. Robert had toured the Parliament buildings in 1870 with the terms-of-union delegation from

British Columbia, but he now wanted a more intimate personal experience with the history of the Senate.

Although Parliament wasn't in session, several secretaries and clerks were happy to talk to the soon-to-be-senator about the workings of parliament. Robert learned that the functions of the Senate were formed in committees and what happened later in the chamber was a consummation of the committee's preparations. His role as senator was to study legislation, scrutinize government spending, and delve deeply into problems of concern.

From one of the clerks, he also learned there was a smallpox outbreak in the city and that his services might be needed. However, the outbreak wouldn't hinder the Adjutant-General's Ball, which was a private affair held each year at the Russell House. The Ball was considered to be one of the largest social events of the season. Robert's was on the invitation list.

The Adjutant-General's Ball was only one of many invitations Robert would receive over the next few weeks. Being of British descent, single and personable, he soon found himself the darling of the Ottawa social set. He would later complain privately to his legislator friends from British Columbia, John Thompson, Hugh Nelson, Edgar Dewdney, and Amor De Cosmos that he was "socially worked to death." He also said that "the girls were so sweet" that he "invariably lost his heart four times a night." (*Dictionary of Canadian Biography*) Despite his late nights, Robert always found time to attend the Anglican Church on Sunday mornings. His family had instilled a reverence for the Sabbath years ago at St. Paul's Anglican Church in Woodstock, which his family still attended.

Finally, the day arrived when Robert was to be sworn in as a senator. That morning, he carefully dressed, his portly figure well camouflaged by a dark, knee-length, double-breasted three-quarter length jacket, nipped discreetly in at the waist. His blue tie, purchased especially for the occasion, was enhanced by a diamond stick-pin. He also had his side whiskers and beard trimmed, but unfortunately there was nothing he could do about his receding hairline.

At the fifth session of the First Parliament, on April 11, 1872, at exactly 2:00 o'clock, Robert William Weir Carrall and four others swore the Senator's Oath of Office. However, Robert didn't make his maiden speech until May 22, 1872, when the Hon. Mr. Alexander Campbell introduced a bill pro forma (in advance) on Bankruptcy and Insolvency. Robert began by saying that he rose with a feeling of embarrassment to address the House for the first time, "especially as he felt compelled to assume a position entirely antagonistic to a gentleman for whose legal acumen and argumentative power, he felt the highest respect."

In a strong, resonant voice, he continued, stating that people who had disposed to act honestly and fairly had been actually driven across the border on account of the harshness of their creditors. He appealed to the House "to give a vote in favor of the necessity of having at all times an equitable means of enabling men to carry on legitimate business and to restore themselves when they have honestly failed." Robert argued that

I need not tell the House that there was a time in the history of the world — not a remote when a condition of impoverishment for debt was in vogue and the word bankrupt was synonymous with the more expressive language of commercial immorality. Not too long ago in this country — people were disposed by the harshness of their creditors. I don't want to see his happen again. Rogues rush in and take advantage of the present law.

On the statute book is a law which enables men to take advantage of their position and become dishonest. I feel it is my duty to vote for its repeal. Now a dishonest man can come into a village and enter into competition with the merchant who had been there for many years carrying on a safe and legitimate business, but who would soon find himself unable to compete with one who started with borrowed capital which he would soon refund and cared nothing for consequences. That trader would eventually get into difficulties, offer his creditors 20 cents on the dollar; and if that was refused at the outset, he would threaten them with an assignment, when probably they would receive nothing. Of course, the creditors would have to yield and a few days later he would come out with a facing advertisement headed "Bankrupt Stock for Sale at 50 per cent below first cost." The natural consequence would be that the honest trader would find himself undersold, and probably in the end irretrievably embarrassed by circumstances arising from an iniquitous law. The speculators who went into business for the purpose of remaining only a few months were the class of persons really protected to vote for its appeal. interest as ever in disposing of their goods, and would be easily deceived as now by unscrupulous traders. I feel the House will give a vote in favor of the necessity of having at all times an equitable means of enabling men to carry on legitimate business, and to restore themselves when they have honestly failed. Unfortunately, there is a law on the statue book which enables men to take advantage of their position. I want the insolvency law changed.

The new Insolvency Law was later passed. However, there were many who felt the bill did not go far enough. "If the law is designed to be in the interests of both creditors and debtors, as it should be, we cannot see why its provision should not be extended as to include all classes — not just traders and farmers" (*Huron Expositor*, March 26, 1875).

Enthused with his success, Robert now proposed to have Dominion Day declared a public holiday, but the idea was immediately cast aside. His colleagues said it just wasn't expedient at this time because the provinces were too new to the harness of Confederation and were resistant to the idea. Nova Scotia was one province that would certainly be opposed as there was still a great deal of discontent in that province about Confederation.

During this Fifth Session of the First Parliament, many issues were debated, including dual representation, the Treaty of Washington, and the Canadian Pacific Railway. Despite a slowing economy, it was expected that the railway would be built although the government did not know the exact cost. However, there were some in the Senate, such as Hon. Mr. Letellier De St. Just, who felt that "the country would be precipitated into financial difficulties on account of our heedlessness in the present."
Robert countered that the railway was a necessity to the union of the country, which would bind two oceans together by links of iron. He said that

> he had confidence in the future of this country, and believed there was no danger whatever of embarrassing our resources in connection with this line. Even if it were to cost much more than anticipated, the country could afford it. The additional population brought into the country would soon enable the Dominion to meet the obligations incurred. He pointed out the superior advantages of the Canadian line in respect to the soil of the country, climate and altitude, as compared with American lines. He referred to the great stimulus the line would give to trade with the countries of the China sea, and the benefit the Dominion would thereby receive. It would develop mineral resources now entirely dormant, and add immensely to the wealth of an already prosperous country.

While politics took up most of his time, Robert did find time to join the Jim Jam Club, an exclusive social club, where he met Joseph Caron, a Conservative MP from Quebec. Like Carrall, Caron was not, nor would be, a high-profile senator, although he proved to be surprisingly effective in mobilizing a police force to counter the Northwest Rebellion.

During this period of growth and change, Lord Dufferin and

his Lady arrived in Canada as the new Governor-General. This coincided with the political expansions of the young Dominion and the settlement of its outstanding political differences with United States. Like Carrall, Dufferin believed Canada should have a free education system that was open to all and that excellence in academic achievement should be recognized.

In the summer of 1872, Canadians went to the polls. Macdonald campaigned vigorously, but a political storm was brewing with Sir Hugh Allan and the Canadian Pacific charter. Macdonald won the election but lost Ontario. However, there was even worse news — Sir George Etienne Cartier was defeated in Montreal and was also diagnosed with the fatal Bright's disease, a disease of the kidneys.

Business interests in the West now required Robert's attention and he returned to British Columbia in early October, on the steamship *Enterprise*. (*New Westminster Mainland Guardian*, October, 1872) A letter from Sir John A. Macdonald was waiting for him in Victoria. "I have come out of the fight very well, on the whole, but lost some constitutes in Ontario, which we could not well spare." The Prime Minister also told Robert that he had appointed Dr. Israel Wood Powell, the man Carrall had recommended, as Superintendent of Indian Affairs.

Carrall must have been thinking of resigning his seat in the Senate as Macdonald implied in his next letter of October 5, 1872: "You must not think of giving up your senatorship. We want you there, and, indeed, you cannot be spared." Macdonald also added a humorous note. "We have great fun with Sir Francis Hincks, asking him every morning "what news from British Columbia," and if he says a word about the Pacific Railway, we charge him with attempting to put the screws to us for the purpose of getting better terms for his own Province." Referring again to Carrall's roots, Macdonald added that the election "was a wise and graceful thing on the part of your people." Robert answered Macdonald's letter on October 13th, thanking the Prime Minister for Powell's appointment. He also said that "he has been touring the province of British Columbia and the people seemed pleased about what is going on in Ottawa." Carrall also said, "I wrote you some little time ago in regard to a personal matter which I hope will receive your favorable consideration." He then added his regard for "Lady Macdonald, Master Hugh, the Colonel and yourself."

On October 27, 1872, Robert wrote another letter to Sir John. In it he says, "I shall without doubt put in an appearance in Ottawa this winter for I have some business that may take me east very shortly." He thanked Sir John for speaking so frankly about the Pacific Railway Commissionership, an executive position with the railway. He continued by saying that he thought that "British Columbia ought to have a member on the Board." He finished the letter by stating that he would serve in whatever capacity that Sir John asked, "in the future, as in the past, to repay you with my devotion to you and, now, the Great Dominion."

That devotion would be tested before the year ended when letters, documents, and even a contract surfaced signed by Hugh Allan and his American associates ensuring them that he would be appointed as president of the Canadian Pacific Railway.

# 10. The Pacific Scandal

On New Year's Eve, Sir John was working late in his office in the East Block. Unexpectedly, George W. McMullen, proprietor of the *Chicago Post* and a shareholder in the Northern Pacific Railway, walked in. McMullen asked Macdonald if the Canadian government was involved in Allan's bid for president of the CPR. Allan had asked McMullen for $343,000 to ensure his election as president. Macdonald said he didn't know what McMullen was talking about. "He came to us. We didn't go to him!" McMullen stated. This, of course, left no doubt that Sir Hugh Allen had not ended his association with his American friends and cast another shadow on the Canadian administration.

Travel was easier now that the Northern Pacific Railway out of Portland, Oregon had been completed. It shortened Robert's trip eastward by a couple of days, and he was able to spend Christmas with his brother, Henry, and his sister Anastasia who had recently married and their families at the Carrall homestead on the outskirts of Woodstock.

Robert was back in Ottawa in plenty of time for the opening of the First Session of the Second Parliament on March 5, 1873. Robert revelled in the pageantry, the choosing of a speaker, and the arrival of the Governor-General. As soon as Lord Dufferin took his place on the throne, he summoned the Gentleman Usher of the Black Rod to usher in the members of the House of Commons. The Black Rod was the symbol for authority to debate in the Upper House, and dated back to early 14th century England. After everyone was seated, there was more pageantry. Then the House adjourned, followed by pleasantries — a buffet and spirits.

The next morning, Governor General Lord Dufferin delivered his throne speech, which set the parliamentary agenda for the coming year. Dufferin began by saying that he was taking office at a "period when the prospects of the country appear so full of promise." Robert almost jumped out of his seat when Dufferin said, "I have caused a charter to be granted to a body of Canadian capitalists for the construction of the Pacific Railway." Robert would have liked the railway issues to be debated at the beginning of their session, but, unfortunately, the Senators got bogged down in mundane issues and they didn't get to the debate on the railroad until a few weeks before the Easter adjournment, which in turn became a debatable issue.

One of the Senate's first debates was about the Senate itself, about its composition, and the means by which the speaker of the Senate was chosen. One senator, the Hon. Mr. Miller, expressed the view that "it was not right and proper that the five provinces should be ignored while one Province had two members of the Cabinet in the Senate." He qualified that statement by stating that he was also against "any policy that might have the effect of lessening the influence and authority of the Senate." Robert entered the debate by stating that "the Senate was the guardian of the smaller provinces and that they above all other sections should object to any policy that would dwarf the influence of that body." He added that he didn't want the Senate to be seen as "a magnificent mausoleum in which moribund politicians might be interred."

While he was one of the youngest members of the Senate,

Robert proved he was well versed in his knowledge of the affairs of the Dominion and the affairs of British Columbia. During a salmon fishing debate, he reminded his fellow senators that although the industry was of recent date, British Columbia salmon was now being exported to Europe, Australia, and other markets around the world. He didn't want to see that market exploited and recommended that salmon fishing on the Fraser River to be scrutinized by the government and the leases protected. "This is bound to be a great industry and the sooner it is fostered and protected, the better," Robert said. He reminded the Senate that the Columbia River had been over-fished and that some canneries had to be shut down. This unsupervised slaughter had caused a dearth of salmon and he didn't want to see this happen in British Columbia.

One aim of Confederation was to standardize the laws across the entire country, which involved changing or modifying provincial statutes. One example was British Columbia's Aliens and Naturalization Act that permitted naturalization after a year's residence. The rest of the country, with the exception of Manitoba, had a three-year residency requirement and the oath had to be administered by a Supreme Court Justice. When the Hon. Mr. Campbell learned of the difficulties in administering the act under the government's regulations, he deferred the issue to the Committee of the House where it could be thoroughly discussed. He then asked Robert for his assistance in redefining the act.

Robert explained that since the province had only districts — there were no counties or townships in British Columbia — an alien desiring citizenship often had to travel anywhere from 100 miles to 500 miles and at considerable cost just to get to a court. He suggested that any magistrate in any court in British Columbia should have the right to hear the alien's oath of allegiance. When one of the committee senators questioned Robert about the shortened period of one year, he replied: "Men in British Columbia live faster — one year being a longer period than three in the Eastern Provinces."

During the session, a private member's bill was brought before the Senate. The Isolated Fire Insurance Company of Canada wanted to change its name to the Isolated Risk Company. Irritated by such a mundane matter, Robert said that he wasn't sure about the company or its capabilities, but it must be pretty good or some of the government buildings would not be insured by them. He voted for the name change.

Outside the political realm, there was much going on in Ottawa during the winter and spring of 1873. Lord and Lady Dufferin organized numerous balls, concerts, dinners, theatrical performances, and plays. Lady Dufferin loved acting and often took the lead role in some of the plays while encouraging others to get involved. It was a well-known fact that Robert loved the theater, but it is not known whether he was involved in any of her plays.

During the spring, the Parliamentary Representatives of British Columbia organized a Provincial Rifle Association and Robert was one of its directors. He loved to shoot and hunt. During his evening hours, the young doctor frequented the Jim-Jam Club, where, with a glass in hand, he defended his actions or non actions in the Senate or told about the deer that got away.

By the time the Easter adjournment came in April, it was evident that Sir John A. Macdonald's government was in trouble. Although the debate on the Canadian Pacific Railway had just recently come to the floor of the Senate, it was certainly widely debated in the newspapers and on the streets. It was alleged that several members of the government had received large sums of money from Sir Hugh Allan during the 1872 election campaign. Meanwhile, the July 1st deadline for starting the construction of the CPR had come and gone and still nothing had been done. It was, therefore, understandable that the people of British Columbia were angry.

The rumblings grew and Sir John went on one of his numerous drinking escapades. Since he and Robert were drinking buddies, his fellow parliamentarians believed Carrall went with him. Without a word to anyone, Macdonald disappeared. Even his wife Agnes didn't know where he was. Robert went to see her as dastardly rumors began to surface. Macdonald had committed suicide; he had run away, he couldn't face his accusers.

On August 10, Macdonald returned just as suddenly as he had vanished. Recognizing that the Prime Minister's health was poor, the Governor-General prorogued parliament for 10 weeks until October 23, 1873. In addition to the railway crisis, the Dominion was now beset with financial problems beyond its control. Earlier in the year, the financial markets in Europe were rocked with the collapse of the Prussian Boom and then in September there was a financial crash in New York.

It was clear to everyone that Macdonald's support in the House of Commons was dwindling and that his government would be defeated in an election. Despite an eloquent five-hour speech, Macdonald could not stop the defections, and on November 5, 1873, the Prime Minister resigned. The next morning Sir John met with his caucus and submitted his resignation to them and asked that they appoint a young leader to take his place. They refused and said that he must stay on as their leader, the position that he had held for 20 years.

Robert arranged a public dinner at the Russell House for Macdonald, which included among those present three parliamentarians from British Columbia: Hugh Nelson, J. S. Thompson, Edgar Dewdney. Amor de Cosmos declined to accept the complimentary invitation as he felt the Dominion government had let British Columbia down with the delay in the starting of the CPR. He wasn't alone in feeling betrayed by the Conservative government. *The Victoria Daily Standard,* November 29, came out with scathing remarks against Robert. "We are not surprised that Dr. Carrall, with all his old Ontario instincts and traditions, acting against this Province, by pure impulse, and worshiping the leader that Sir Hugh Allan bought, but we are surprised to find that he had the presumption to call himself a representative of British Columbia." Robert responded on December 5 with the promise that the moment he believed that he was not representing the views of his people, and the interest of his Province, that moment he would send in his resignation.

*The Senate in the 1870s during Dr Carrall's tenure.*

*Robert Carrall's sister, Anastasia.*

# 11. Second Fiddle

Senator Alexander Mackenzie was appointed as Canada's second Prime Minister on November 5, 1873. He was a dour, pragmatic, hard-working Canadian of Scottish birth, who disapproved of alcohol and certainly the drinking habits of Senator Carrall. One of Mackenzie's first duties as Prime Minister was to prorogue parliament and call an election. After the January 22, 1874 election, the Conservatives became a minority in the Lower House, but since the senators were appointed, they retained their majority in the Senate. Sir John A. Macdonald, now the leader of the minority Conservatives, cautioned his colleagues to take a low-key position but keep "strictly and silently" upon the defensive.

The First Session of the Third Parliament of the Dominion of Canada opened on March 26, 1874. The next day Governor General Lord Dufferin outlined the new government's priorities and stated the problems of the previous government in his throne speech. He said that "the previous government having failed to secure the prosecution of that great enterprise, you will be called upon to consider what plan will be best and most speedily provide the means of trans-continental communication with British Columbia." He also referred to the Chief Engineer's report, the progress of the CP surveys, and the railway office fire that destroyed maps, plans and papers.

The country was in a financial crisis, which Mackenzie's government contended was due to Macdonald's spendthrift habits. One of Mackenzie's ministers was heard to say to say that right now "Canada couldn't even pay for the axle grease of the locomotives much less build a railroad for them to run on." Robert heard at the Jim Jam Club that the Mackenzie government had already sent J. D. Edgar to British Columbia to negotiate a new agreement for the construction of the CPR. He didn't know, however, that Lord Carnarvon from the Colonial Office in England had laid down the terms.

The Conservatives knew that business would be done differently now, but Robert was caught flatfooted when one of the government's new senators announced that a Mixed Land and Water Trans Continent Connection with British Columbia was now in place. "Do I understand you to say the government has prepared a scheme?" Carrall asked Senator Scott, one of the new members of the Senate.

"Yes, a scheme for the connection of this country by land and water with British Columbia," Scott replied. "I thought you gentlemen were aware of it. It was prepared from observations made by Sir Stanford Fleming."

"I was not." Carrall answered.

"It is generally known, however," Scott replied. Fleming was a distinguished engineer and surveyor who strongly favored a new railway to the Pacific.

When one of the senators became ill with smallpox, the *Ottawa Times* published an article blaming the disease on Ottawa's sanitary conditions. Surprisingly, the Senators defended the young city, which had spent one-half million dollars on the water department and was now completing a half million dollar sewage system. They contended that this was an amazing accomplishment for a city that only 46-years ago was forest.

The lax enforcement of the vaccination law to prevent smallpox became an issue for Robert. He believed in vaccinations but knew that in poorer areas, like those in Montreal, doctors had promulgated the notion that vaccinations were a poisonous operation and should be discontinued. One senator wanted a law to be passed that would force all children to be vaccinated, but he was informed that vaccinations came under local law while quarantines came under federal law. During the debate, it was recommended that a committee be formed to study the issue and that Robert be a member of that committee.

When an adjustment to a constituency's boundaries bill came to the senate, many felt it should be rubber-stamped and passed into law, simply because it had been unanimously passed in the House of Commons. Robert disagreed, arguing that they should look at the facts separately. But after days of debate, the only change made to the bill before it was passed was the removal of the word "now."

The Vote by Ballot and the Qualifications Election bills were hotly debated. The conclusion was that there should be a uniform franchise for the whole Dominion, but the franchise should be sufficiently elastic to suit the whole country. When the qualification of candidates became a contentious issue, Robert got to his feet. He said that "as long as a man was honest and had capacity for public business, it was of little consequence as to the amount of his credit at the bank or the value of the real estate he possessed. Neither should it matter if the candidate was Canadian by birth or by naturalization."

With the country now in a financial decline, testy questions were being asked in both the Senate and House of Commons. Did the government still intend to honor the terms of Union with BC, committing £100,000 to BC for construction of a dry dock at Esquimalt or would that be reduced? Why didn't the government hire qualified engineers and surveyors from British Columbia instead of hiring them in the East and then having to pay to send them West?

Just a few weeks before the government was to be prorogued, the Senate finally began its debate on the Canadian Pacific Railway. Accusations flew across the floor. One Liberal senator had the audacity to hint that the only reason BC wanted the railroad was for the convenience of its nine men in Parliament. Robert jumped to his feet. He said that he looked upon the building of the Pacific Railway as "the great agent in work of European emigration and work that would make the Dominion a competitive nation with our neighbors in the south of this continent, in trading with the rest of the world." He contended that, in time, Canada would have the lion's share of the carrying trade between East and West and the money derived from this trade would help pay for the railroad. His arm raised, his fist clenched, he shouted, "The Canadian Pacific will build up a great future for Canada!" The Upper House adjourned without anything being settled.

The Second Session of the Third Parliament of Canada began on February 11, 1875. With a heavy heart, Senator Carrall took his seat on the opposition's side of the Senate Chamber. Macdonald's Conservatives were no longer in power.

He listened attentively to Lord Dufferin's throne speech, which outlined issues that needed to be debated: measures enforcing prepayment of postage on letters, uniform rates of interest on business transactions, and the extreme cost of divorce. In Robert's mind, these were mundane issues, especially when such larger issues like the Canada Pacific Railway and a better Insolvency Law needed to be debated.

Robert had to agree that the creation of the North-West Police force, 500 men and a quartermaster, was a positive step forward. Mobilized by his friend Caron, the force would not only keep the peace in the North-West Territories, but reduce the need for the military. Another positive bill sponsored by the Liberals was the creation of the Supreme Court of Canada, essential in the Canadian system of jurisprudence and the settlement of constitutional questions.

Unfortunately, friction in the Lower House spilled over into the Senate. Amor De Cosmos, the BC's representative in the House of Commons, whom the *Ottawa Free Press*, March 15, 1875, referred as "an egotistical torpedo liable to explode at any moment," made disparaging remarks about Robert and Sir John A. Macdonald. In a humorous tone, Robert responded, "He is known to be fond of change, and not being able to change anything else, changed his own name." Before taking up residency in British Columbia, De Cosmos's name had been William Alexander Smith.

Robert wholeheartedly supported the motion to grant a subsidy to the British Columbia Steamship Company for the carrying of mail to and from Victoria and San Francisco. He also informed his fellow senators that an agreement had been reached at a Postmaster's Convention that the mail would go through United States to other parts of Canada at the rate of our own domestic postage in closed bags free of charge.

Although not married, he took a stand on the divorce bill. "In this country where Church and State are entirely separate, it is improper to import theological arguments into the discussion." He believed that the Divorce Court, like all other courts, ought to be made as accessible as possible to everybody. Speaking about the case that was before the House, Robert brought laughter to the floor when he said that "it was extremely unfair that the wife of the petitioner had not been heard in her own defense, and that in the future her children would at least be able to say that it was a Scotch verdict, that is "Not Proven." (*Ottawa Free Press*, March 15, 1875)

Robert brought the northern Columbia border line issue before the Senate on March 29, 1875. The land in question, now owned by United States, was a narrow strip stretching from the 56 and 101 parallel between the Coast Mountains and the Pacific Ocean. When Russia had owned this land, the miners had easy access to and from via the Stickeen River, which was navigable for approximately 160 miles from its mouth to the source in the northern interior of British Columbia. Now, there were a military outpost, custom officers, and toll bars along the first 60 or so miles of the Stickeen.

During the winter, Robert had met many of the miners in Victoria where they were buying their supplies for spring. These men, though migratory, were generous, loyal and law-abiding, and wanted to be free of American harassment on the Stickeen, the chief entrance to the gold districts. Other waterways, whose sources were in Canada, emptied into the Pacific. The miners also wanted to know whether they would be operating under British Columbia mining laws or those of the North-West Territory. Robert asked what progress had been made in negotiations for the settlement of this boundary line between British Columbia and Alaska.

Senator Scott, speaking for the Government, said that the "gentleman who acted for Great Britain when the Treaty of 1825 was made, knew nothing about the subject." Three parties, Great Britain, the United States, and Canada, were now consulting and the boundary line between the United states and Canada was being finalized. But at this time, the Northern British Columbia and Alaska line was almost indefinable. He felt that after all the surveys were complete, the governments might be disposed to look on the matter favorably. (Boundary Debate minutes)

Robert was in favor of the organization of a Court of Appeal in Canada. He believed that it was desirable to have some tribunal to which disputed questions between local legislatures and the Dominion Parliament could be referred, but was opposed to abolishing the final appeal to England. It had taken almost four years for the best legal minds in Canada to elaborate this bill, but its passing depended on one's interpretation of the British North America Act. (Supreme Court Bill Debate)

The first major legislation confrontation between the Senate and the House of Commons came when the Senate rejected a bill passed by the Lower House on a railroad from Esquimalt to Nanaimo in British Columbia. Ironically, Sir John A. Macdonald had voted for the railway, which was viewed "as a sort of peace offering on account of the inability of the Dominion to carry out the agreement made with British Columbia at the time of union." (*Huron Expositor,* April 9, 1875). Robert said that he "believed in British Columbia, but there was a want of confidence in Canada — a suspicion that they would never even attempt to construct the Canadian Pacific Railway." However, "for the peace, good order and welfare of the whole country" he said he would vote for the building of the Esquimalt to Nanaimo railroad." Lord Dufferin prorogued parliament on April 9, 1875.

The Third Session of the Third Parliament began on February 10, 1876. Lord Dufferin, who had recently returned from a trip to England, read the throne speech the following day. It touched on the depression, the near-completion of the railroad between the Maritimes and the Province of Ontario, and the settlement of fisheries compensation provided in the Treaty of Washington. It didn't mention that Prime Minister Alexander Mackenzie had also been to England and was offered a knighthood, which he had turned down.

After the usual replies to the throne speech, the Senate got down to business, but it wasn't until the following month that the Robert got the opportunity to make his motion.

It was a different man who got to his feet on that March 20, 1876. In the past Robert's witticism and lightness of manners had often turned off his more somber and older colleagues. Today, however, there were no quips, no humorous banter, no jests. He was completely serious.

He made his motion:

That the construction of the Pacific Railway having formed the principal condition upon which British Columbia entered the Canadian Confederation, every reasonable effort should have been made by the Government of the Dominion to satisfy the people of that Province that faith would be kept with them; but this House regrets to find that whilst incurring, or ready to incur, immediate expenditures of several millions of dollars not needed, or of doubtful utility, the Government has failed to proceed vigorously with the construction of our great national inter-oceanic railway, which is so essential the material advancement of all the Provinces of the Dominion, as well as to the early consolidation of political and social union among the whole people.

As he gave his reasons for making the motion, he became very tense. He said that the same men who opposed British Columbia's entry into confederation were the same men who now opposed the building of the railway. Their reasons were money-related: they wanted to preserve the fur trade or their appointments came from Downing Street. A few were emissaries from United States who were pressing for annexation, especially after that country's purchase of Alaska.

Robert emphasized that the three men who had come from British Columbia to negotiate the terms of union were fiercely loyal to British Columbia and to England. A graving dock at Esqu...alt, permission to allow their tariffs to remain in force for a ten-year period, and, of course, the construction of the CPR within a 10-year limited were all part of those terms of Union. However, the latter was not an absolute.

The railway as a national necessity. Certainly, without it, there would be no immigration to the West. Robert compared the importance of the building of the CPR to Wolfe's victory at Quebec. He considered the failure of Sir Allan's scheme to build the railroad a national calamity because it was the prelude to the fall of Sir John A. Macdonald's government.

Once in power, the Mackenzie government had sent J. E. Edgar to British Columbia to negotiate a new deal, but his mission failed. British Columbia then sent its premier to Ottawa to negotiate with the Prime Minister for a satisfactory solution to the stalemate. He, too, failed. British Columbia then appealed to the Imperial Government in Britain for redress, which resulted in the Carnarvon Compromise. The compromise had suggested that "the original terms of union would stand, that the number of survey parties would increase and the Esquimalt-Nanaimo railway would be built, regardless of whether or not it would become part of parcel of the trans-continental line." Also, the compromise suggested that not less than $2 million should be expended annually in BC construction.

Certain government members had disparaged BC at every turn. The Prime Minister had once said in a speech that BC had no right to representation in the House and that they represented nobody but Indians. Others said the people of BC were leeches, pariahs, and blood-suckers, who were sucking the milk out of Ontario.

In a calm, controlled, but forceful voice, an angry Robert said that there was "no man who surpassed him in loyalty to the national flag" and "if the present government didn't do what was right, they would do their best to put them out and get men who would do them justice."

Hours later, a slight amendment to the motion was made by Hon. Mr. Hawthorne: "an effort should be made without increasing the taxation of this country... to satisfy the people of that Province that faith will be kept with them." This was followed by a motion to the amendment that acknowledged the Dominion's obligation to construct the railway with the utmost speed, with due regard to the country's other financial obligations. The Senate was divided but finally the amendment was carried.

During this long debate, Carrall often refuted the remarks made in the press. While he might be an insignificant member of the House, he wanted to be accurately quoted. He felt there "should be some line of demarcation between license and liberty of the press and they should be governed by these rules or principles."

The House adjourned on April 12, 1876.

*Governor-General's gala in the gardens at Rideau Hall, social events Robert Carrall frequently attended.*

# 12. The Return of Sir John A.

After clearing his desk of correspondence, Robert arranged his itinerary for the summer and fall. In early June, he was off by way of New Brunswick and Nova Scotia to the Centennial Exhibition in Philadelphia, the largest exhibition ever held in North America. Canada was one of the exhibitors. In addition to the new Corlis engine, which Robert thought could be used in BC, there were displays of wood and minerals from around the world, including New Brunswick. Ontario presented a well-documented history of their education system from public school to university. Robert was gratified to see that the Baptist College at Woodstock had been linked to the University of Toronto in the documentation of the Ontario system of education.

In the medical field displays, there was a new orthopedic apparatus for broken limbs and a display of the well-known and much-used Carter Family Medicines of pills, salves, and bitters. The Total Abstinence Fountain display didn't interest him until he read the name of Charles Carroll of Carrollton, his grandfather's brother, on the base of one of the statues. He was also surprised to see the name of another relative, Archbishop John Carroll, on another of Abstinence Fountain statues.

After several more days at the exhibition Robert was off to the West. He was sorry he was going to miss Sir John A.'s picnic stumping in Ontario, especially when the leader of the Conservatives was going to visit Oxford County, but he had to be in British Columbia before Lord and Lady Dufferin arrived for their visit to the province on August 16, 1876. The main thrust of the visit was to assure the people of British Columbia that they were wanted in Canada and that the Dominion government would honor their commitment to them.

When the Dufferins came ashore at Esquimalt on August 16, they were greeted by Sir James Douglas and several dignitaries. Shortly afterward they went by carriage to Government House in Victoria, where a grand reception was held. In his after-dinner speech, Lord Dufferin thanked the province for its warm welcome and stated that the Dominion placed a high value on British Columbia and its people. However, Amor De Cosmos, BC's representative in the House of Commons in Ottawa, refuted Dufferin's words: "We prefer separation to union with a government that offers money for principle and asks us to sacrifice a solemn agreement between England, Canada and Columbia."

During the next few days, Lord Dufferin had a congenial and informative meeting with Dr. Isaac Wood Powell, superintendent of Indian Affairs, the man Dr. Carrall had recommended to Sir John A. Macdonald for this important position. Powell told the Governor General that his worst problem with the Indians was whiskey and the men who sold it to them.

After a journey along the entire British Columbia coast, the Dufferins landed at New Westminster, the gateway to the Fraser River. From there, they journeyed by steamer up the Fraser to Fort Hope, where they were greeted by Mr. Dewdney, another of the province's representatives in Ottawa. From Fort Hope, the royal couple traveled in their specially-built coach north by road and paused for some time at Hell's Gate to view the roaring waters that were gushing through the Fraser canyon. It was then on to Lytton and Cache Creek and later to Kamloops, where another reception was held. Lord Dufferin later told Robert that he would have liked to have traveled farther north to the Cariboo, but time wouldn't permit.

The royal couple's last official duty was Lady Dufferin's gala ball, which was held on September 18th, at Government House. Of course, Robert was one of the 500 guests who attended.

The Conservatives came to Ottawa for the opening of Parliament on Thursday, February 8, 1877, with a renewed sense of vigor. They wanted revenge for the Pacific Scandal that had brought down their government, and there were tiny slivers of hope for them in the Governor-General's throne speech. "During the recess I visited the Province of British Columbia and had much satisfaction in becoming acquainted with the people of that interesting portion of the Dominion and with the climate and resources of their province." He mentioned the Exposition in Philadelphia and commended Canada on its displays in mining, agriculture, and manufacturing. He hoped that Canada would go to the next world's exhibition at Sydney at New South Wales in a couple of years.

The Governor-General mentioned that while Canada's treaty with her Indians was costly, it was cheaper and more humane compared to other countries. He didn't specifically mention the massacre of General Custer and his men at the Little Big Horn or the hundreds of Indians that had come north to Canada, although the inference was there.

Robert was pleased with Lord Dufferin's speech because it outlined several topics that related directly to British Columbia. Since his motion and the debate of last year, Robert had gained stature in the Senate and was quite willing and able to take on the senior senators.

Later, in debate, Robert asked why Mr. Fleming, Engineer-in-Chief of the Pacific Railway, had gone to the Colonial Office and Naval Officers in England for their opinions regarding a terminal for the CPR on the Pacific Coast. He said he had learned of this, not from government documents, but from the *British Colonist* newspaper in British Columbia. He also wanted to know why Esquimalt and Stamp Harbor, two of the best harbors on the Pacific Coast, were not included in that list of harbors. "British Columbia knows her waters just as well, or better, than the Colonial Office," he said. Robert then outlined the different routes that had been mentioned, their advantages and their disadvantages. He again emphasized that there was no mention of Esquimalt or Stamp Harbor. "But if this government did not advise Mr. Fleming to make this application to the Colonial Office, who did?" he demanded. He didn't get a satisfactory answer.

Robert later questioned the costly expenditures of deepening the waterway and upgrading the lock at Fort Francis: "Americans receive more benefit from our canals than the people of Canada." He then quoted a letter in his possession that referred to the exclusion of Canadian vessels from the navigation of certain waters in the United States: "When our government was building the St. Francis canal, our vessels were obliged to tie up at Albany, being refused the use of the Hudson River."

One of the most animated debates of the entire session was caused by a betting bill to prevent gambling and pool selling— pool selling being the betting of as much as $20,000 by one bettor on one particular race. However, with the way the bill was worded, the average man who bet a very small sum would be liable equally with the gambler who bet thousands. One senator said that to remove betting from horse racing would do away with the amusement altogether, and there were few enough amusement in this country as it was. Robert said he had received numerous letters contending that the bill would affect people it was not intended to reach — horse owners, race track owners, and the average bettor. He said he would only vote for the bill if amendments were made. He didn't add that he loved horse-racing and wasn't averse to placing a small bet himself.

The question of the failure of certain insurance companies came to the floor of the Senate, failures which affected the small investor. There were only three failures, two by rascality and one by poor business acumen, and this one had now amalgamated with a much larger company. Since these were American companies, Robert said he was "in favor of any legislation that would encourage native (Canadian) companies." (Insolvency debate)

The Fourth Session of the Third Parliament was prorogued on April 28, 1877.

Now free from some of his political duties, Robert visited his late-sister's step-daughter, Amelia Gordon, who was now living in Ottawa. During the past few years, he had taken an active interest in the Gordon family's affairs. Amelia's barrister husband, John, had died suddenly of cerebral apoplexy (stroke) on December 6, 1871, leaving her with five children aged 4 to 14, a mortgaged house, and little money. Shortly afterward, Mary Jane, her step-mother and Robert's sister, had died. On April 10, 1873, Amelia's father, Sheriff John MacDonald, had succumbed to a fall. It had been a terrible period for the Gordons as they reeled from one bereavement after another.

With the country was in recession, Amelia's oldest son, John Macdonald, who was now head of the Gordon household, was finding it difficult to find a job, especially one that would help support his family. Uncle Bob, as he was affectionately called by the Gordon children, stepped into the breach. Through his friendship with Sir John, he was able to find MacDonald suitable employment in the office of the Hon. David Laird, Minister of the Interior.

After ensuring the Gordon family was all right, Robert was off to the West and his duties in British Columbia. If anyone noticed his stomach was bloated, they assumed he was just putting on weight. Only a few very close friends knew he was having very serious health problems.

Robert was back in Ottawa for the opening of the Fifth Session of the Third Parliament on February 7, 1878. Lord Dufferin read the throne speech. It would be his last as he and Lady Dufferin were being replaced in the fall.

In his speech, Lord Dufferin referred to the disastrous fire that had swept through the city of St. John, New Brunswick on June 20 last year. He said "what it had taken the people 90 years to build, the fire had swept away in three hours." The fire took everything in its path: government buildings, churches, banks, stores and dwellings, leaving approximately 15,000 people homeless. Now, seven months later, with the help of their own insurance money and $20,000 from the government, St. John was being restored. There was also great inconvenience caused by damage to the bridge over the St. John River, resulting in a break in the railway communication system between Halifax and San Francisco.

In the ensuing debates, when one of the senators questioned the amount of tax per head paid by the smaller and newer provinces, Robert reminded the senator that "British Columbia pays nearly three times as much taxes per head into the Dominion Treasury, as any other province in the Dominion."

Later that month, the Senate discussed the salmon fishing industry. Robert made a motion that "all offers or tenders that have been received for leasing of the exclusive right of salmon fishing and netting in the Fraser River, be laid before the House." He, and many others, including the Marine and Fisheries Department, were concerned about over-fishing on the Fraser River and the other rivers of the province. Robert held in his hand a memorandum, signed by the other government representatives of BC — Cornwall, Roscoe, Dewdney — who contended that BC's salmon industry had exported more than half a million dollars in its first year. However, the industry needed conservation and protection if it was to survive. During the year, there were three or four distinct species of salmon that ascended the river at different times and that each had a different breeding season. The industry wanted a close time that would prohibit fishing from 8:00 a.m. Saturday to midnight on Sunday, allowing the fish two whole days and a night to ascend the river free from interference. They also wanted the size and width of mesh of the fish nets to be restricted: the canneries and fish curing establishments compelled to bury or utilize their fish offal, and well-paid bailiffs to enforce the law. "To us in British Columbia, fishing is really a question of bread and butter," said Robert. "Therefore, I invite at the attention of the Government to seriously consider this matter."

He made it clear that his motion did not affect the native peoples who were allowed to catch fish and shoot deer out of season. British Columbians felt that if any attempt was made to stop them the natives would not understand it and there would be problems like those occurring across the border with Sitting Bull. The motion was acknowledged and passed on to the Marine and Fisheries Department for immediate enactment.

When it was again suggested again the railway route should go north to the Peace River, Robert admitted it was a good idea, but not at this time. The character and country did not justify the construction of a railroad through it at the present time. The construction of the Pacific Railway debate continued on into April 1878 and when another survey on the Pacific terminus was suggested, Robert jumped to his feet. "After an outlay of several million dollars and after seven years of work, the government ought to be in a position to declare where the terminus on the Pacific Coast should be!" He wanted work on the terminus to commence without further delay.

Several senators contended that a transcontinental railway would never pay its way. This was repudiated when figures were brought forth to show that in 1875, the Union Pacific Railway, a trans-continental railway below the border, had an $8 million profit. Robert accused the government of tremendous stupidity. "Seven years, enormous sums of money have been frittered away — yet all we have to show for them is some miles of telegraph, wire and piles of steel rails scattered throughout the country, corroding for want of use." Then, using his drama talents, Robert walked slowly to the table in front of the speaker, took a bag from his pocket and, holding his arm high so everyone could see, emptied its contents of oxidized iron rust onto the table. The debate was quickly adjourned.

During the next session, Liberal Senator Scott made a motion for "the advisability of abolishing the office of Receiver General." He claimed most of that department's work was done by the Finance Department and they didn't need two departments doing relatively the same thing. He said that the Office of Minister of Justice was over-burdened, and his motion would divide that work with a new Department of Attorney-General. Robert believed that it wasn't wise to tinker with the system just before an expected election. The present system, which in his opinion was working well, was based on the British system that had checks and counter-checks in every department, and all monies expended were double receipted.

With the prospect of an early election, the *Globe* newspaper went on the attack, printing scathing articles about the Conservatives, especially about their leader Sir John A. Macdonald. Owned by Senator George Brown, the *Globe* accused Sir John of being "thoroughly laid out" at a ceremonial dinner on Friday, April 16th. After reading the article, Robert took action. The next morning, he moved for an adjournment of the present debate in the Senate, stating that he wanted to give a personal explanation to the Globe article. "I want to address a subject that has pained me more than anything since I became a member of the Senate of Canada." He said referring to the newspaper article. "I was at the ceremonial dinner which was held in the salon below the House of Commons. Sir John had eight oysters with a glass of sherry and water."

"How were the oysters served?" someone quipped.

Ignoring the quip, Robert continued, "Hector Cameron and I were with him until 6:00 o'clock this morning when we went for breakfast." Robert then accused the absent Senator Brown of trying to mould the policy of the Dominion, hiding behind the impersonality of a *Globe* editor by writing articles that belittled the leader of the Conservatives. Robert then quoted lines from a Longfellow poem:

Lives of great men all remind us
We can make our lives sublime
And departing leave behind us
Footprints on the sands of time.

He finished his narrative by adding, "I beg to withdraw my motion for the adjournment of the debate."

The Senate was then asked to amend the Act representing the election of members to the House of Commons. The gist of the bill was to prevent retired civil servants from running in an election for a seat in the House of Commons. However, the consensus was the Senate had the right to interfere in qualifications or disqualifications of parties elected to the Commons, only so far as it did not interfere with the rights of the people.

On May 10, 1878, Governor General Dufferin addressed the joint Houses of Parliament for the last time. He said that many things had been accomplished during the Fifth Session of the Third Parliament. British Columbia had established telephone communication with the rest of Canada. A definite line between Alaska and British Columbia on the Stickeen River had been finally adopted, and the Dominion now had undisputed sway over the northern half of the continent.

Dufferin didn't say that he knew the country would go to the polls before too long. However, Prime Minister Alexander Mackenzie's government wobbled along until August when an election was called. There seemed little doubt in his mind whom would form the next government of Canada. With a new National Policy, the prospect of a good harvest, and a reviving economy, there seemed little doubt that Sir John A. Macdonald would form the next government.

# 13. Dominion Day

In early June, after a private talk with Sir John A. and a visit to his surrogate family, Robert was ready to leave for the West. On the way he intended to make a side trip to Woodstock to visit his brother, Henry, who now lived on the family homestead.

In October, 1878, word came by telegraph that Macdonald's Conservatives won with a landslide victory. Robert was elated. But that elation was tempered with the fact that he, himself, was very ill. In early November, Robert checked himself in the Royal Columbian Hospital in New Westminster, and word quickly spread that he was gravely ill. In fact, one newspaper reported his death.

Sir George Walken, the Premier of British Columbia, heard the news and he checked with Robert's doctor. On November 29, 1878, Walken wrote privately to Sir John A.: "I'm afraid poor Carrall's days are numbered. Liver, kidneys and stomach are all badly affected and the doctor considers his recovery hopeless."

However, reports of Robert's demise were premature. While he was in the Royal Columbian Hospital at New Westminster, he received a letter from his nephew in Ottawa. Whether this letter caused him to check out of the hospital or whether he had decided to do so anyway is not known. The letter was from

John McDonald Gordon, Amelia Gordon's son. After the usual salutation, J. M. got to the point:

I know you have done a great deal for me, but you are the only one I can ask to do this for me. I have been struggling along for years trying to live on promises received from both Mr. Laird and Wills that I should be promoted and each and every time those promises have been broken. During last session I had to work in the evenings to try and keep up with my work and the Colonel recommended that I should receive an increase and an assistant. The Minister promised both and put in a friend of his at the same pay as I got and made no alteration to mine. In the summer he promised me, instead, he appointed two new clerks with a higher salary than mine, and this is the way things have gone all along. I should not have cared so much if only I had myself to support but having Mama and the others on my hands, my pay is not enough to make both ends meet. Now I want you to write Sir John and ask him to give me an appointment of $1,200 or $1,000 a year. Urge it as strongly as you can. I could manage on a $1,000 with the usual increase, but try and do what you can for me.

Robert immediately wrote to Sir John A. enclosing J. M.'s letter:

The enclosed is from McDonald Gordon of your Department. Colonel Dennis will give you the merits of the case. Please ask the Colonel and oblige. I expect to be over very shortly. With warmest regards in the great victory and for the holiday greeting for Lady Macdonald and yourself.
R.W.W. Carrall

This letter, barely decipherable, is dated, Victoria, December 19, 1878. It is not known if Robert arrived in Ottawa before Christmas or shortly after the holidays.

Parliament opened on a cold February 13, 1879. The speaker

of the Upper House was appointed and several new senators were sworn in. The members of the Lower House then withdrew to elect a speaker for the House of Commons. The next day, February 14th, the Marquis of Lorne, John Campbell, delivered the throne speech.

The new Governor-General's speech was fairly short. He expressed his "gratification at being selected by Her Majesty to this high office and the kindly manner in which the people of Canada had accepted her daughter , his wife, Princess Louise." He then outlined the government's accomplishments and priorities. He told parliament that he had been at the Great National Exhibition in Paris where many Canadian products had been on display. They had drawn much attention and he felt sure Canada' would derive much trade from the exhibition. He said that he had been informed that the United States had paid their fishery claims to Britain and that both Canada and Newfoundland had benefitted from the payments. Unfortunately, the contagious pleura-pneumonia cattle disease in United States was prohibiting the importation of American cattle into Canada. The Marquis concluded his address stating that "it is the purpose of my government for the vigorous prosection of the CPR and to meet the reasonable expectations of British Columbia." After the Governor-General's speech, both Houses adjourned so that everyone could enjoy the pleasantries provided for the occasion.

When Parliament resumed on Monday, February 17, 1879, the Hon. Clement Cornwall, another Senator from British Columbia, gave a lengthy and glowing reply to the Governor General's throne speech. There was no hint that Cornwall wasn't happy with British Columbia's entry into Confederation, a fact that would later catch Robert and others by surprise.

Several of the senators gave glowing reports about the former government of Alexander Mackenzie. However, Robert was not of one of them:

I had not intended to say a single word....but I consider it a duty to myself and to the Province I represent to endorse and supplement what has fallen from the lips of the mover of the Address. Although many of the members of the late government are among my personal friends, I consider that they were unfit to meet the emergencies which have arisen during the last five years. It was unfortunate that during a great commercial crisis, they happened to hold the reign of power. They have left behind a number of monuments from Halifax to Victoria in the shape of steel rails. (First Session Fourth Parliament)

Senator Armand, one of the 24 senators from Quebec, followed Robert's lead, claiming that the previous government had not been friendly to Quebec. He said that Quebec now had no representation in the Lower House, and he felt that long-standing members not currently in the House should be consulted regarding policy and change.

The day ended on a sad note when the Hon. Alexander Campbell asked that an address of condolence be presented to Queen Victoria at the death of her daughter, Princess Alice, Grand Duchess of Hesse-Darmstadt. Princess Alice had died of diphtheria on December 14, 1878 at her home at Darmstadt by the Rhine.

The much-anticipated annual Governor-General's Ball at Rideau Hall was held on February 19th. The ball was not an invitation-only event; anyone who could "afford the dress" was welcome to attend. Carriages lined the circular drive bringing parliamentarians, merchants, river captains, and others. While they waiting to be presented to the royals, everyone admired the great hall with its gold velvety drapes, pale blue walls, and gold trimmed arches. However, it was the huge chandelier in the centre of the ballroom that was truly awe-inspiring.

Clearly feeling better after his severe illness, Robert attended the ball with Amelia Gordon on his arm. When it was their turn to be presented to the royals, Robert bowed and Amelia curtseyed. Shortly afterward, the dancing began. Governor-General Campbell danced the first dance with Agnes Macdonald, while Sir John A. waltzed with Princess Louise.

As was customary, a silk cordon separated the vice regal party from their guests. Ottawa's elite was shocked when Princess Louise ordered that it be taken down. Some later joked that this might have been a mistake — before the ball was over, a drunken band member fell off his chair, the daughter of the tailor had danced with the Governor General's aide, and Robert accidentally stepped on the train of Princess Louise's gown.

The next morning the senators were back in the Upper House debating on the issue of the restriction of cattle with pleura-pneumonia. Robert, whose family background was in agriculture, was knowledgeable and well-informed. He considered that all necessary precautions had been taken, and since the disease hadn't shown up in Chicago or to the west, the ban on shipping cattle could be lifted. He also pointed out that the railroads were suffering from lost revenue.

Robert also entered the debate on the appointment of Captain Richard Layton as Warden of British Columbia's penitentiary. The Mackenzie government had removed Layton, a man known by Robert personally, from that position because he was of a different party and appointed someone less suitable and less qualified. Now BC wanted Layton returned to that position. After much pressure, Layton was re-appointed.

When the government wanted to open communication between York Factory and the North-West Territories, all that most senators knew about York Factory was that it was 660 miles south of the arctic circle and could only be reached by navigation through Hudson Bay. Many had never even heard of this Canadian outpost. When Robert enquired as to how long the passage was open, he was told only four to six months of the year. One optimistic senator felt that a day not far distant would find that York Factory at the mouth of the Nelson River could be on par with St. Petersburg, Russia. Both lay within the arctic circle. Robert wasn't that optimistic. However, with the land around York Factory thought to be rich in minerals, he voted to send an expedition to the area to explore the land. (Navigation of Hudson's Bay debate)

A bill was introduced to the Senate that would provide for the salaries of two additional judges of the Supreme Court, replacing the present county court judges. Robert reminded his colleagues about the vast area that the judges were asked to cover in the course of their duties and that they incurred greater expense as a result. He agreed that the expenses of the judiciary in BC were greater than other provinces in proportion to the population. He felt, too, that the judges who were to be pensioned due to the change in the judicial system could take on other occupations and that the country would benefit from their services. He concluded that pensions, however, should be restricted to those advanced in age. "We must bear in mind that the cost of administrating justice is greater in a sparsely settled country than in a densely populated area." However, County Court Judges in British Columbia also acted as gold commissioners, collectors of revenue, Indian agents, etc., and performed in a manner that had given almost universal satisfaction. He could see no reason replacing them with judges more learned in the law. County Court judges are " vigorous men, in the prime of life, quite competent to conduct the courts of the country of which they have an intimate knowledge, and I cannot see any necessity for superannuating them at present, or replacing them by new judges who would be a greater expense and not cognizant of the wants of the country and people for whom they would have to adjudicate."

Controversy arose about the building of the Coteau Bridge across the St. Lawrence between Canada and the United states. Some of the senators felt that the bridge would allow rich corporations to monopolize trade between the two countries.

Robert had no objection to the building of the bridge and pointed out that the Mississippi River was bridged in various places and that these bridges enhanced the flow of trade, not hindered it. He said that he had always looked at the railway as a national highway and decisions regarding it should not be influenced by sectional or personal feelings.

During this period, a senator complained that his speeches weren't being accurately published in the press. Since Robert was on a contingent committee, he knew that debates were being printed according to their value and to what was interesting to subscribers. "As mine never appear in any newspaper they cannot be of value," he quipped lightly. He had recently learned quite a bit about printing and costs: any senator who wanted to present a private bill to the House had to pay the legal, printing, translation, and distribution costs, plus a minimum fee of $200.

On March 26, 1879, the Speaker of the House announced that Robert had asked leave to introduce a private member's bill to make Dominion Day a public holiday. When no major objections were heard, Robert introduced Bill H: An Act to make the first day of July a public holiday by the name of Dominion Day.

After the bill was read, the Senate continued on with other business. It wasn't until April 2, 1879, that Robert moved for the second reading of his Bill H and explained to the Senate his reasons for presenting the bill:

I have always had a great desire to be the father this bill, and I find that already, on the other side of the House, the idea has been taken up, to deprive me of the honor of consecrating the birth of the Dominion. There is no question about it; I undoubtedly was the first to propose that the first of July should be a statutory holiday. Eight years ago, I made the proposal but it was thought inexpedient to pass such a measure because some provinces were new to the harness of Confederation. The bill was withdrawn.

I think we should fix upon some national holiday and educate the rising generation to revere a flag under which we live. I believe Dominion day in some of the provinces is a public holiday, but it is not a fixed holiday.

I have always loved the Dominion dearly. I helped to found it. I have worked since with all the energy I possessed by vote and voice to consolidate it.

I think we should have one day which should be observed throughout the Dominion as the anniversary of Confederation. Like the mighty empire of Rome, some part is always in rebellion. British Columbia is restive and irritated. Now is the time to legislate the Dominion into one harmonious whole.

I have no desire to make a spread-eagle speech, but I speak my own feelings, claiming to be a patriotic Canadian, descended from a race of patriotic Canadians — one of the oldest families in Canada.

Senator Campbell began the debate saying that it was a good time to pass such a bill, that the feeling of dissatisfaction had passed away in all the provinces. However, shock ran through the Senate when Clement Cornwall, Robert's colleague from British Columbia, departed from protocol and spoke against Bill H. "Eight years has passed and the iron bond which was to unite the country is not real — British Columbia's union with the Dominion has not been consummated."

Senator Havilland of Prince Edward Island was angry. "Senator Cornwall, in his address to the throne speech congratulated the county on the position of everything, and he is now saying the union of the Provinces is only nominal (existing in name only). Our future is brighter now than when we were a number of disintegrated provinces."

One Nova Scotia senator questioned the loyalty of British Columbians and Robert's suitability in presenting such a bill, especially since there were so many dissenters in his province. Robert angrily replied that if he had his way all dissenters would be put in jail. As to his own loyalty, "I shall do my utmost to hold the provinces together as one Dominion, ocean to ocean."

Several senators were concerned about the affect of taking away a working day. They claimed there were too many holidays already and that they were costly for business. Still another senator proposed that maybe it be a holiday under provincial jurisdiction only, not a federal holiday. However, one of the Nova Scotia senators felt that it should be a federal holiday, that "we should unite in making Dominion day a statutory holiday under one flag, one constitution, and with good government, we will grow and prosper and become the brightest jewel in the British Crown." The debate dragged on until Senator Levin from Londonderry proposed an amendment that "the second reading of the bill should be postponed for six months. Robert was furious, but a vote was on the amendment was taken — 36 for the second reading to be given now, 25 for the second reading to be postponed.

Robert then read the Bill H for the second time. It was then sent to the Committee of the Whole, who decided that the bill would be read for the third time on the Monday next. However, on April 7, 1879, on one of the most important days of his life, Robert was absent from the House, and Senator Aiken "moved concurrence in the amendments made in the Committee of the Whole." The motion was agreed to and the Dominion Day bill was read for the third time. Despite the infrequency of a private member's bill passing the Senate, the Dominion Day bill passed after its third reading. The bill was then sent to the House of Commons with this message attached: "The Senate has passed a bill entitled "An Act to make the first day of July a Public Holiday by the name of Dominion Day" to which they desire the concurrence of this House. On April 9, 1879, Hon. James Cockburn, member of West Northumberland accordingly read the Bill for the first time, seconded by a Mr. Robinson. It was then ordered to be read a second time at the next sitting of the House of Commons.

On April 15, at the end of a long night session, the Bill was read for the second time. It was then sent to Committee, where another bill on statutory holidays was also being considered. Since it was ridiculous to have two bills on the Statute Books, it was agreed only the Dominion Day would go before the House, where it would be debated. On April 28, 1879, word was carried back to the Senate that this House had passed the bill without amendments:

> Throughout the Dominion of Canada, in each and every year, the first day of July, not being Sunday, shall be a legal holiday, and shall be kept and observed as such, under the name of Dominion Day.

Canada would celebrate its first Dominion Day holiday on July 1, 1879. Robert was elated and seemed to gain strength from the bill's success.

When the Pacific Railway Policy came before the Senate again, Robert inquired as to why construction of the railway on the Pacific Coast had been delayed. He argued that at the time of Confederation the building of this railway was not merely for colonization purposes, but also as a portage between Europe and Asia. "My constituents feel like hauling down the flag, but the commencement of construction would have a tendency to quiet their irritation which is endangering our political existence." He was assured by Senator Campbell, the Conservative leader in the Senate, that this announcement would come in a few days.

During the next few weeks, Robert's voice was often heard on the Senate floor; in fact, he seemed to have a renewed sense of vigor. He now wanted to know whether the Government intended to appoint an Inspector of Telegraphs for the Province of British Columbia this year. He then proceeded to give the topography of British Columbia and a brief history of the telegraph in the province, which had been purchased from the

Western Union Company. He described the waters between Vancouver Island and the mainland as rough and pointed out that the lines were often cut by the strong currents slamming the telegraph lines against the rocks. On the mainland, the only people who could inspect the 600 miles of line were the telegraph operators who were merely lads. Hence according to Robert, the need for inspectors.

There was much speculation on May 8, 1879, when Robert was absent from the Senate's session. He was supposed to introduce a bill to repeal the Indian Act of 1876 and make a motion to present the Governor-General with all correspondence between the government and the Commissions of the Indian Reserves in British Columbia. Instead, the bill and motion were introduced by two Senate colleagues. Where was Dr. Carrall? The answer was simple. On May 8, 1879, Robert married Amelia Gordon, whom he had met when his sister Mary Jane married Amelia's father, Sheriff John McDonald. She had been only eight years old at the time and he had been immediately smitten.

Senator Carrall was absent for the rest of the First Session of the Fourth, which was prorogued on May 15, 1879.

---

THE NEW DOMINION

Oh! Land of the Maple and Beaver
We love to hear thy praises Anew.
With Canada join'd, say who can
    e'er sever,
A country and flag firm and true.
Chorus
Hail new dominion
Thou glorious and free
Soon may the empire
Span from sea to sea

Thy sister Columbia, whose
    resources are many
Would improve under thy fost'ring
    care.

Then say come with us thou land
    of the west,
We'll make one great father land.
    Chorus

For Confederation thy strength,
    Dominion thy name,
Thou bright and shining star.
May wisdom, power and concord
    combine,
To make thee a giant so grand,
While from ocean to ocean thy
    empire extends,
In dominion, our own dear
    father-land.
    Chorus

# 14. A Life Too Short But Well Lived

Nothing is heard of Robert Carrall until late August when the social column of the Woodstock *Sentinel Review* printed a few lines about Dr. Carrall and his wife, Amelia, saying only that they were visiting family and friends in the area. Actually, the Carralls were staying at the family homestead, the three-storey buff brick house where Robert was born, two miles west of Woodstock. The news of their arrival was overshadowed by the forthcoming visit of the Governor-General, the Marquis of Lorne, and Princess Louise, who were on a tour of Ontario and would be in Woodstock on September 18, 1879.

Unfortunately, Robert's health was deteriorating, and he and Amelia were only seeing family and a few close friends. The two were often seen walking hand-in-hand around the homestead now owned by Robert's brother, Henry. It was an impressive place with well-kept lawns, a fish pond, and orchards. From the bluff overlooking the Thames River, they could see Carroll's Grove and his grandfather's house. They talked reverently of the older man who had instilled such love of country in his children and grandchildren.

Although Robert hated the thought of leaving Amelia, he was ready for the transition that as a doctor he knew was near. He had achieved much in his life as a doctor and as a politician. He knew, too, that a railroad would soon connect his beloved Canada from sea to sea. And his dream of having the nation celebrate July 1st, the Dominion's birthday, as a public holiday was now law. He was content.

On September 19, 1879, Senator Robert William Weir Carrall died at the age of 40.

*The Royal Columbian Hospital in New Westminster where Dr Carrall was diagnosed with terminal disease.*

*Memorial to Senator Robert Carrall at the Anglican cemetery on Vansittart Avenue in Woodstock, graced with the inscription: "This monument was erected by his personal friends in the Senate and Commons of Canada."*

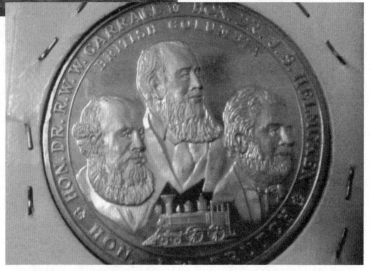

*Commemorative coin honoring the founding fathers of British Columbia -- Robert Carrall (left), John Sebastian Helmcken (center), and Joseph R. Trutch (right).*

# Epilogue

There have been many tributes to R. W. W. Carrall, MD, over the years. Some have been forgotten in the pages of history. Others are still solid reminders.

In 1971, a commemorative medal was produced by the Victoria Numismatic Society commemorating British Columbia's entry into Confederation in 1871. The reverse side of the medal bears the likeness of Hon. Dr. Robert William Weir Carrall, a native of Woodstock, Ontario and Legislative representative for the Cariboo. The centre figure is Hon. Dr. John Sebastian Helmcken spokesman for Vancouver Island and the old-time settlers. On the right is Hon. Joseph W. Trutch, a civil engineer and the first Lieutenant-Governor of British Columbia. All three men negotiated the terms of union that brought British Columbia into the Dominion of Canada.

Shortly after Dr. Carrall's death, a street in Vancouver was named in his honor — Carrall Street, a main thoroughfare that connects with Hastings Street. Recently, a greenway has been constructed beside the street for bicycles and pedestrians.

# Sources of Information

Library and Archives Canada
National Archives of United States
National Museum of Civil War Medicine
British Columbia Archives
McGill University Archives
Ontario Provincial Archives
Oxford County Archives
Perth-Stratford Archives
Victoria Numismatic Society
Beachville Museum,
Brantford Public Library
Goderich Public Library
Ingersoll Public Library
Thamesford Public Library
Woodstock Public Library
Woodstock Historical Society
Masonic Lodge — Nanaimo
Masonic Lodge — Woodstock

# Photo Credits

Page 2 : Library and Archives Canada
Page 15: Music Library and Archives Canada
Page 22: Map Registry Office (old records), Woodstock
Page 24: Commemorative book on Woodstock, circa 1901
Page 25: Woodstock Museum Archives
Page 32: Woodstock Museum Archives
Page 33: Old St. Paul's Church, Church Archives
Page 34 Commemorative book on Woodstock, circa 1901
Page 53 ff: National Archives, Washington, DC
Page 66: Royal British Columbia Museum
Page 75: Royal British Columbia Museum
Page 86: Royal British Columbia Museum
Page 93: Royal British Columbia Museum
Page 94: Postcard, Niagara Falls
Page 102: Library and Archives Canada
Page 115: Library and Archives Canada
Page 116: Woodstock Museum Archives
Page 126: *Toronto Star* Supplement
Page 149: Royal British Columbia Museum
Page 150: Author
Page 151: Victoria Numismatic Society